*40 favourite walks*

The author and publisher have made every effort to ensure that the information in this publication is accurate, and accept no responsibility whatsoever for any loss, injury or inconvenience experienced by any person or persons whilst using this book.

published by
**pocket mountains ltd**
The Old Church, Annanside,
Moffat DG10 9HB

ISBN: 978-1-907025-97-6

Text and photography copyright © Neil D'Arcy Jones 2024

The right of Neil D'Arcy Jones to be identified as the Author of this work has been asserted by him in accordance with the Copyright, Designs and Patents Act 1988

A catalogue record for this book is available from the British Library

Contains Ordnance Survey data © Crown copyright and database 2024 supported by out of copyright mapping 1945-1961

All rights reserved. No part of this publication may be reproduced, stored in a retrieval system, or transmitted in any form or by any means, electronic or mechanical, including photocopying and recording, unless expressly permitted by Pocket Mountains Ltd.

Printed by J Thomson Colour Printers, Glasgow

# Introduction

Essex is a county full of surprises. Not only is it one of the largest counties in England by population and area, it also has the country's longest coastline after Cornwall, some of which can be explored through the walks in this guide.

In recent years, Essex has been much maligned, with an abundance of clichés and stereotypes in popular culture, some of which are not unfounded. For better or for worse, no-one could ever accuse Essex of existing in 'the M25 bubble' and the contrasts between the downright gaudy and the glorious is part of what makes the county inspire such loyalty and such love.

In this guide, you'll see Essex in all its glory while also getting the chance to appreciate its multiple layers: oil refineries and ports overlooking large stretches of saltmarsh, country estates drifting into industrial estates and pounding motorways flowing beneath dense forests that thrum with wildlife. Somehow, as the wilder pockets and corridors weave seamlessly in and out of the bustling built-up areas, it works.

For those who think they know Essex, the walks in this guide will make you think again.

## History

The Kingdom of the East Saxons, or Essex as it came to be known, was according to legend first established in 527AD after Aescwine defeated Octa, king of Kent.

Historically, the lands that became Essex were some of the most important in the country well before that date. In 43AD, the Romans established their first capital in Camulodunum (now Colchester), where two ancient British tribes, the Trinovantes and the Catuvellauni, had made their strongholds. Some 17 years later and the Queen of the Iceni, Boudica, was razing Colchester to the ground.

The area which forms the county as we know it today was gradually developed in the later Anglo-Saxon era, before the Norman invasion in 1066. With its close proximity to the new capital and centre of government in London, Essex continued to play an important role in the country's affairs. Castles were built at Colchester, Hedingham, Rayleigh, Pleshey and Hadleigh. Around the same time, the Forest of Essex was legally made a Royal Forest, beginning a long-running association between the kings and queens of England with the Forests of Epping and Hatfield.

One particular event of note in the county's history was the Peasants' Revolt of 1381, perhaps the first true 'grassroots' beginnings of democracy in England, rather than the Baron-led Magna Carta of 1215. It began in several Essex villages, including Bocking, Brentwood and Fobbing, after a new tax was imposed on an already impoverished workforce.

Later noteworthy events included Queen Elizabeth I's impassioned 'I have the heart and a stomach of a king' speech to her troops at Tilbury Fort before the Spanish Armada in 1588, and the Siege of Colchester in 1648 during the Civil War. Essex was also unfortunately the centrepoint of the notorious Witch Trials of the 1640s, led by Manningtree's Matthew Hopkins.

In more recent times, Tilbury was where the *Empire Windrush* docked with around 800 migrants from the Caribbean looking for a new life in the UK, one of whom was Sam Beaver King, the founder of the Notting Hill Carnival and the first black mayor of Southwark.

### Wildlife

In 1967, one of the greatest nature books ever written was published – *The Peregrine*. It's an account by J A Baker of a year spent following a pair of peregrine falcons close to his Chelmsford home. There's every chance that walkers will get to enjoy their own 'Baker' encounters while exploring the routes in this guide, whether that's through an occasional buzzard or red kite swooping high on the thermals above or the myriad waders and seabirds – oystercatchers, plovers, little egrets and cormorants – that gather up and down the Essex saltmarshes.

With such an intensively urban and industrial landscape, especially in the south of the county, it's the pockets of nature and the huge range of wildlife found in them that proves so irresistible.

Epping and Hatfield, among other areas of woodland, continue to cultivate and protect the county's tree population, with some dating back more than 1000 years. Epping itself is home to 55,000 ancient trees, more than any other site in England. The forest is also one of only three sites in the country where knothole yoke-moss grows, as well as being home to fallow deer, lizards, frogs, butterflies, 10 different species of bat and a beetle that only lives off ancient trees.

Dig deeper into the county and there are plenty of other rare delights waiting to be discovered – from the Fisher's estuarine moth at Walton-on-the-Naze to the shrill carder bee on Canvey Island.

### Walking, weather and topography

Essex may be one of the flattest counties in the country, with its highest point a modest 147m, but there are still a few workouts to be had – from climbing cliffs at Walton, Dovercourt and Southend to sweeping down into valleys at Danbury, Wrabness and West Bergholt. That said, as the Netherlands is to cyclists, so Essex provides the perfect terrain for those who like their paths steady and level.

At various times of the year, though, those paths can get overgrown and muddy, so take care to equip yourselves accordingly and, strange as it may seem, at times you could be miles from anything as civilised as a shop, so take plenty of provisions to sustain you on your travels. On most of these walks,

# Introduction

you'll be able to find a quiet scenic spot to stop and enjoy a picnic, but you will also discover some very pretty pubs, teashops and cafés along or near the routes where you can sample the local fare. By the coast, at West Mersea or Leigh-on-Sea for instance, this might include delicious freshly-caught oysters or other seafood served from seaside shacks.

In terms of weather, St Osyth, near Clacton, is the driest place in the UK with an average rainfall of 20 inches per year and Shoeburyness, near Southend, comes a close second. If evidence of its relatively low rainfall and high levels of sunshine were needed, it can be seen in the thriving vineyards, including ones at Burnham, Mersea and Bardfield. However, don't be caught out without a raincoat on the Essex coast where sometimes it can feel like it has its own micro-climate distinct from the rest of the country.

## Travel

Despite Dr Beeching's best efforts to close as many branchlines as possible in the 1950s, Essex still has a comprehensive rail network. Consequently, many of the walks in this guide either start from a railway station or are linear walks between two, some with spectacular estuary views as you make your way back to the start. When the train doesn't quite cover the relevant area, there is usually a good bus route nearby.

With its large population and proximity to London, the road network is pretty exhaustive too, with plenty of major routes such as the A12, A120 and A13 providing quick and easy access to all four corners of the county, as well as to the walks in this guide.

Many of the routes start near dedicated car parks or where there is on-street parking, for which there may be a charge.

## About this guide

This guide is designed to give a snapshot of Essex and the variety of walking it has to offer, taking in everything from urban and industrial heritage to more natural attractions tucked away down winding estuaries, along riverbanks and through acres of woodland. There's even a route that takes you quite literally out to sea.

Times given for each walk are based on an average walking speed of 3.5km per hour, with a bit of extra time added so that you can read the guide and look at a map when required. The sketch maps in this guide are for illustrative purposes only and in many cases it would be useful to have the relevant OS Explorer map given at the start of each walk.

Several of the walks cross farmland grazed by sheep and cattle, so take care to close gates and keep any dogs on a lead.

If this guide has inspired you to explore more, it is well worth checking out some of the county's long-distance paths, including the Essex Way, the Saffron Trail and St Peter's Way.

The Stort Navigation ▶

**You might think being on the capital's doorstep** would dominate the West Essex corridor that runs from Saffron Walden to the Thames Estuary but, as the walks in this chapter illustrate, it does not.

In the north, Thaxted and Saffron Walden offer walkers a chance to step back to a bygone age when classical music ruled the airwaves and the plough and ox ruled the furrows. To the south, Thorndon Country Park is a haven of wildlife and serenity. Between them are plenty of vibrant rural environments to explore – from the canalside habitats around Harlow to the vast expanse of Epping Forest that sits loud and proud on the outskirts of one of the largest and most dynamic cities in the world.

This area is very nearly the perfect introduction to a county that continues to offer up surprises around each river bend, sea wall and country lane.

# West Essex

**1 Saffron Walden** — 8
Visit one of the largest mansions in England and tour the historical treasures of this medieval market town

**2 Thaxted** — 10
Enjoy a circular walk around a lovely rural town with some unexpected industrial and musical heritage

**3 Hatfield Forest** — 12
Step back in time and imagine the Norman kings and lords who once hunted deer in this unique place

**4 Harlow Mill to Roydon** — 14
Look out for moorhen, kingfishers and otters on this linear towpath walk from station to station

**5 Chipping Ongar** — 16
Make the pilgrimage to the oldest wooden church in the world and return through woodland and meadow

**6 Epping Forest** — 18
The last stop on the Tube's Central Line is the start point for this hike around one of the county's most famous forests

**7 Snaresbrook to Buckhurst Hill** — 20
Stroll through an ancient woodland corridor, formerly part of a royal hunting forest on the edge of London

**8 Thorndon Country Park** — 22
Dive into a deep dark wood and immerse yourself in nature on this tour of a popular country park

# Saffron Walden

**Distance** 6km **Time** 2 hours
**Terrain** town pavements, footpaths, country tracks **Map** OS Explorer 195
**Access** regular buses to Saffron Walden from Bishop's Stortford, Stansted Airport and Haverhill

Originally just called Walden, meaning 'Wooded Valley', this historic market town got its more 'modern' name in the 16th century when due to its climate and soil it became the perfect place to grow the saffron crocus. While the town has many attractions, including the largest turf maze in England and the remains of a 12th-century castle, the jewel of them all is the palatial Jacobean mansion of Audley End House – one of the finest examples of its kind in the country.

Start from Swan Meadow car park by following the blue signs into the town centre. With the Cross Keys Hotel in front of you, turn right and then right again down Abbey Lane. Carry on past the Almshouses on your right until you reach a grand old gatehouse of the Audley End Estate and a set of iron gates. Go through and head on up, bearing diagonally left towards the estate wall and another gate which leads out onto Audley End Road. Turn right to the entrance gate of the house, run by English Heritage, where there are fine views of the buildings and surrounding parkland, although if you want a really good look around, it's worth paying the entrance fee to go inside.

Cross the road, where the entrance to the miniature railway and enchanted fairy

# SAFFRON WALDEN

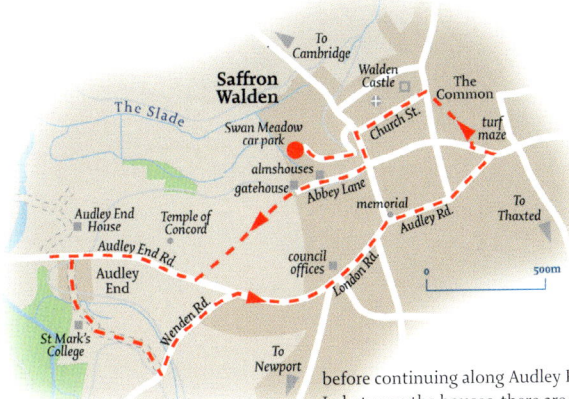

and elf walk is located, and then double back up to the signpost for St Mark's College and a pair of five-bar gates. This leads you between the pretty rows of whitewashed cottages built to house the workers of Walden Abbey, once located where the house is now.

Carry on down the lane, keeping left at the fork, to head past outbuildings on your right and attractive tree-lined fields on your left. When you reach Wenden Road, turn left to head up the hill. At Audley End Road, cross over and then turn right.

Keeping the brick estate wall on your left, walk back into town, going over a couple of mini-roundabouts and past the impressive Old Saffron Walden Hospital which now houses the offices of Uttlesford District Council. Carry on until you reach the war memorial where you should take great care crossing over before continuing along Audley Road. In between the houses, there are views of the town's church, which has the tallest spire in the county. The road eventually leads down to a triangular junction, where you go left. After passing a terrace of flint houses, there's a gap which leads you to an iron bridge. Cross this to the common.

To your right is Saffron Walden's famous turf maze, but you need to walk in the opposite direction, heading diagonally up towards the ruins of the 12th-century Walden Castle. This was a stronghold of the overly-ambitious Earl of Essex, Geoffrey de Mandeville, who rebelled against the Crown and died from an arrow wound while besieging another castle in 1144.

Cross onto Church Street and walk down past St Mary's Church, before turning left back down the High Street, where in a few steps you'll be back outside the Cross Keys. Opposite is Park Lane which leads back to Swan Meadow car park.

◀ The gates at Audley End House

# Thaxted

Distance 8km Time 2 hours 30
Terrain town pavements, footpaths
(some muddy), country tracks
Map OS Explorer 195 Access buses to
Thaxted from Saffron Walden and
Great Dunmow

Thaxted has a quintessentially English village vibe but with a few surprises in store – from an unusually impressive church for such a small place to the magnificent timbered Guildhall dating back to the 15th century. Both make sense when you realise Thaxted was the centre of a thriving cutlery industry during the Middle Ages. More recently, it has been the centre of musical excellence, thanks in large part to Gustav Holst who lived and worked in the town.

Start from the car park in Margaret Street, turning right out of the car park and then left at the end of the street onto the main road. By the pub on the corner, cross over, taking care of traffic, and walk down Watling Lane. This winds round to the right, past a couple of colourful thatched cottages. Keep left and you'll shortly see a grass track leading down to some gardens on your left. Stay to the left of the tree but hug the hedgerow as you descend to the bottom, where you head left and then right, across a bridge and into a field. Carry straight on up into another field and then through a gap in the hedge into another one, which leads across to a collection of houses in the distance. This is Cutlers Green, its name a reminder of Thaxted's cutlery history.

Cross the road, keeping the green on your right, and carry on past a small pond to reach a fork in the road, where you need to keep left. This takes you through Loves Farm and past a watertower onto a small track. At the bottom of this, you

◀ Thatched cottage in Cutlers Green

should see a blue waymarker pointing to a footpath on your left.

Take this, ignoring the footbridge on your right to walk straight along the wide grassy path that leads into a field. Turn right and then at the next gap turn right again, up past a small copse of trees, until you reach the top of the track close to some mounds of earth, which archaeologists believe were old mill mounds.

Head left between the mounds and follow the waymarker ahead that directs you into the woods. This path bears right and down into a gully which can be quite waterlogged after wet weather. Out of the woods, cross the road to the small country lane that winds past fields, fishing lakes and then finally into the little hamlet of Folly Mill. Just past the grand white houses with black-painted outbuildings and over the River Chelmer, the road crosses the long-distance path, the Harcamlow Way, where you turn left.

Follow the riverbank, crossing a couple of stiles, until you get to a dense hedgerow where there's a signpost for the path heading left. This takes you up onto the main road, where you cross and double back on yourself until just after Park Style Cottage, where the Harcamlow Way continues on your right. This takes you back up into the town past John Webb's Windmill, a fine example of a brick tower mill, built in 1804.

Keeping the mill on your left, head back into town, through the kissing gate and past some almshouses to the front of the church. Bear right through the churchyard and down Stoney Lane, where you'll see the old Guildhall and, a little way down the main road on your right, the house where composer Gustav Holst lived from 1917 to 1925. Turn left up Watling Street, then right down Bell Lane and you're back at the car park.

# Hatfield Forest

**Distance** 11km **Time** 3 hours 45
**Terrain** woodland paths, country tracks, footpaths (some muddy), fields
**Maps** OS Explorer 195 and 183
**Access** buses from Braintree, Stansted Airport and Bishop's Stortford to The Green Man pub, Takeley Street, 150m from the Flitch Way

Founded by Henry I in 1100AD, Hatfield Forest is home to more than 3500 species of wildlife, as well as a lake designed by Capability Brown. Circumnavigating part of the forest's 1000 acres, this walk ticks off three long-distance paths – the Harcamlow Way, the Three Forests Way and the Flitch Way, which follows the former railway line from Braintree to Bishop's Stortford.

Start from the National Trust's Shell House car park near the café and lake, taking the footpath which sets out in a southwesterly direction. Past some trees, there's a stretch of grassland leading off into the distance. Carry on to the top and, as it opens out, bear left down the broad coppice until you reach a large field with a line of trees in the distance.

Off to your right there's a path that leads down to the South Gate. Keeping inside the forest, bear right through the trees until you reach another gate. Turn right here, the path bringing you back up in a northerly direction until you reach a T-junction. Turn left, go through the gate and carry on along the narrow tree-lined path. Follow it round to a road bordered by attractive houses, including a picturesque thatched cottage. This is where you pick up the Three Forests Way, turning right up a track to pass a corrugated outhouse and brick shelter before reaching a bridge with iron railings nestling in some hedges up ahead.

Cross the bridge and climb through a small patch of woodland to reach a lake,

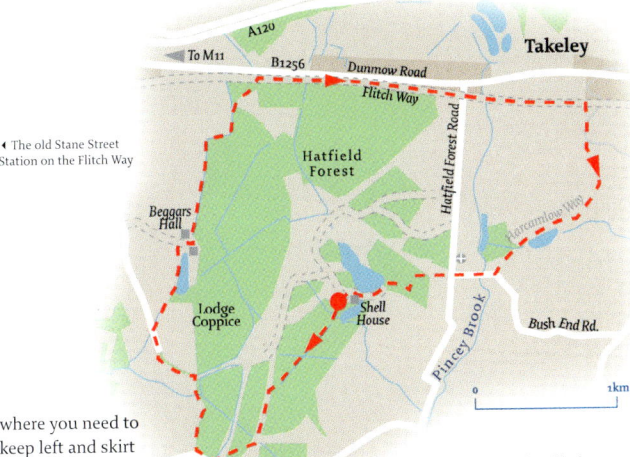

◀ The old Stane Street Station on the Flitch Way

where you need to keep left and skirt the water. Reaching the end of the lake, go over a stile and head across a track towards a country lane where you turn right.

This leads into the gravel parking area of Beggars Hall, but if you look carefully you'll see the National Trust sign and a gate at the right side of the building ahead. Go through the gate and turn left.

This path edges alongside the forest to your right and some farmland on your left until you reach another open area of grass. Head diagonally across to a gate, through which you'll find the Flitch Way. Turn right and carry on along the old railway line for around 2km. If you want to cut your walk short, there are gates leading back into the forest which you can use to return to the lake.

Just past some new-build housing on your left, your route on the Flitch Way intersects with the Harcamlow Way. Head right through the gap and, keeping the line of trees on your left, swoop down and around the field, passing a gate and a lake behind some woodland. Up ahead, you'll see a narrow gap in the woods where the path leads you on through a small copse, after a while heading uphill and left to emerge in a field. Turn right towards a stile up ahead. Cross the field to another gate and go right down the country road.

Up a slight incline, at the T-junction, cross the road and return to the forest. Head into the trees and carry straight on, ignoring the track leading to a house on your right. As you come out of the woods, you'll see the lake. Head left along the path towards the brick building where you'll find the Forest Café, behind which is Shell House car park.

# Harlow Mill to Roydon

**Distance** 9km **Time** 3 hours
**Terrain** canal towpath, town pavements
**Map** OS Explorer 174 **Access** buses to Harlow Mill from Epping and Bishop's Stortford and trains from Cambridge, Bishop's Stortford and London Liverpool Street; this is a linear walk, returning to the start by train

It doesn't get further west than this, with the walk crossing the Hertfordshire border as it follows the towpath along the River Stort Navigation. Navigable since 1769, the canalised part of the river has 15 locks in all. With the high-rises of Harlow peeping over the trees, it's a welcome haven for wildlife where moorhens hide in reedbeds, kingfishers swoop beneath sagging willows and a stretch just downstream from Hunsdon Mill Lock is home to a bevy of otters.

Start from Harlow Mill Station and take the ramp from the car park up to the main road, where you turn left. Continue on this road until you have crossed the bridge over the River Stort, then head left down to the towpath below. This is the first of six locks you'll pass – if you're lucky you might get to see a narrowboat going through one.

Carry on along the towpath as it loops alongside the waterway through canopies of thick oak and hornbeam with the occasional elder, ash and willow. It's so enclosed in parts, the path feels separated from the rest of the world, the only hint of civilisation being the occasional glint of a warehouse or the chimney of a glass factory towering into the sky from the industrial estate to the south.

Occasionally, the navigation splits around small islands offering up secluded mooring spaces, and there are several bridges you can cross to get a view from the other side.

As the river emerges into a more open

# HARLOW MILL TO ROYDON

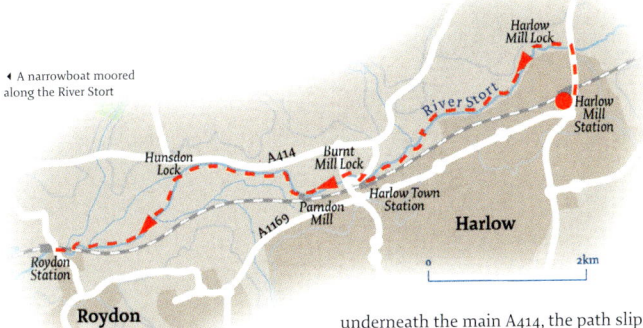

◀ A narrowboat moored along the River Stort

space, the footpath crosses the bridge and continues downstream towards Harlow Town. The 'New Town' is much in evidence with its blocks of housing as well as the Grade II listed Town Station. One of many 'New Towns' built after the Second World War to ease the overcrowding in London due to the Blitz, Harlow is well known for having one of the most extensive cycle networks in the country, as well as Britain's first pedestrianised shopping precinct.

Eventually, the path comes out into a parking area by the Town Station. This is Burnt Mill Lock, where you need to take care following the path on the narrow section next to the lock, passing the lockkeeper's cottage before climbing the steps to the road above.

Cross the road, then head right to walk back down to the towpath. Dipping underneath the main A414, the path slips back into a gentle meander before arriving at Parndon Mill, where people have been milling flour from grain for almost 1000 years. Past the lock, cross back over the river and head right along the towpath to reach the next lock, Hunsdon Lock, where you go back over to the other side. This part of the river intersects a wide expanse of meadow either side with thick clumps of hedgerow in several places. As the river stretches round to the right, you can see the Cambridge mainline.

At the next lockkeeper's cottage, head right and then over a bridge back onto the towpath, which sweeps left under the railway line. You'll see several modernist riverside properties across the water as you come into the village of Roydon, along with some more traditional. As the path comes out onto the road, go right and take care crossing the railway line to the station, where you can take a train back to the start.

# WEST ESSEX

# Chipping Ongar

**Distance** 6km **Time** 2 hours
**Terrain** town pavements, footpaths, country tracks, fields **Map** OS Explorer 183
**Access** buses to Chipping Ongar from Chelmsford and Brentwood

The highlight of this walk is the Church of St Andrew in Greensted, the oldest wooden church in the world. Chipping Ongar has its own delights, meanwhile, among them the Epping Ongar heritage railway, the longest of its kind in Essex, the earthwork remains of an 11th-century motte and bailey castle and more than 70 listed buildings, including Wren House, an 18th-century timber-framed building with original shop window.

Start from the Pleasance car park by Chipping Ongar Library and cross the main road to Banson's Lane which leads down to a farm track forming part of the Essex Way. Cross the bridge over the brook and go through the gate, ignoring the path off to your left to instead carry straight on up the hill. At the end, cross the wooden bridge into the clump of trees, going over a little track to the path ahead. This sidles along woodland to your right and a pasture on your left before coming out on a pretty little lane where behind the tall hedge on your right is what is claimed to be the oldest wooden church in the world. The timber planks of Greensted Church date back to 1060, but excavations revealed two earlier buildings dating back to the 6th and 7th centuries. Open most days, it's well worth stepping inside its small beautifully beamed and red-carpeted interior.

From the churchyard, return to the lane, head right and walk down and around a

# CHIPPING ONGAR

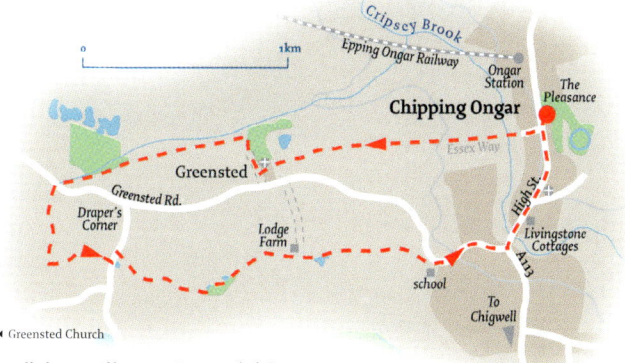

◀ Greensted Church

small cluster of houses. On your left in about 100m, the Essex Way will take you along more grassy meadows. Go through a gap and into another field, carrying straight on over the track at the end. Here, the path becomes more enclosed with trees and tightly knitted blackthorn.

The path eventually leads to a country lane, where you head diagonally across to your left to pick up the Essex Way as it leads into another field. Bearing left and uphill, the path then nips into the trees, through a kissing gate and up into a small field with clumps of large trees on one side and a line of manicured hedged trees on the other. At the end there's another kissing gate to go through, but where the Essex Way heads right, you need to turn left. This path leads to a road named Draper's Corner after the hanging of a man called Draper at the corner with Greensted Road – his ghost is said to still haunt the place.

At the road, head to the left and around the back of the cottage garden where a footpath follows the edge of a field.

Through the first gap, continue keeping the hedgerow on your right to a wider gap where you switch over to the adjoining field, now keeping the hedge on your left. Keep an eye out for a narrow path on the left, which leads into a small copse. This path soon bears round to the right out of the trees and into another field where you walk down through more gaps between fields. At the end, you come to a gate and a stile by the entrance to a school.

Turn right onto Greensted Road and follow it as it snakes around to a roundabout where you go left up Chipping Ongar High Street. Halfway up, look out for the Livingstone Cottages, where the explorer and missionary David Livingstone lived briefly before he set off for Africa, and then further up Wren House, a 16th-century shop with 18th-century features, behind which is the 11th-century St Martin's Church.

Continuing on the High Street, carry straight on to eventually find yourself back at the Pleasance car park.

# Epping Forest

**Distance** 9.5km **Time** 3 hours
**Terrain** town pavements, woodland paths, country lanes, fields
**Map** OS Explorer 174 **Access** buses to Epping from Harlow; Central Line to Epping Underground Station

Bearing in mind how populated Essex is, it's perhaps surprising how many forests it contains. Epping, like Hatfield, is a throwback to the royal forests, preserved so the monarch could hunt deer, but in recent years, they've become a welcome respite from city living. This walk has the glorious joy of twice crossing one of the busiest roads in the UK, the M25, and at one of those points you'll have absolutely no idea that you're doing it.

Start from Epping Underground Station where the Essex Way begins, although this walk goes in the opposite direction – taking the Centenary Walk instead.

Leave the station building at its main entrance and turn right. Across the road immediately after the car park exit, you need to take a narrow footpath between fences. This leads round to the left and then up a set of steps to Centre Drive, where you turn left. Keep on this road until you get to Western Avenue where you turn right to follow it as it curves to the left before taking a footpath that leads right into woods. Carry on along this path, following the yellow arrows in and out of patches of woodland before it emerges onto a common with the Epping High Road up ahead. Turn left and continue through the trees with the road off to your right.

Eventually, this brings you out onto the Epping Cricket Club pitch which, uniquely, is built on top of a tunnel carrying the M25. Turn right and take care

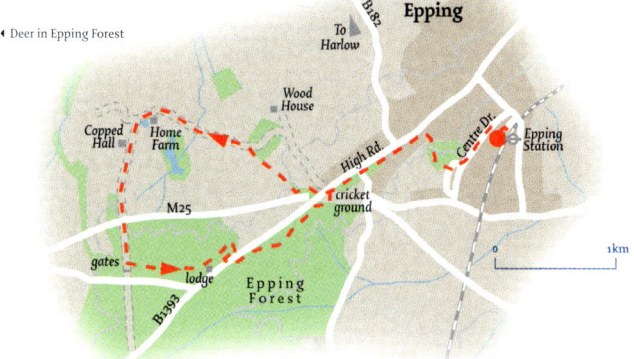

◂ Deer in Epping Forest

crossing the very busy main road, before heading left where you'll see a footpath heading off to the right. This path leads up to the roof of the tunnel and then round to the right and left alongside the motorway itself, albeit separated from it by a big bank and fencing.

This path heads into fields and, though it veers away from the M25, the rumbling is audible throughout the walk. At the end of the field, go through some woods to a country lane at the end, where you turn left.

This lane goes up and around to the left, past a pretty duckpond and towards a little collection of estate cottages. Before you reach them, go through a kissing gate on the left which leads up to Copped Hall, an impressive Georgian house now run by a trust and currently under restoration.

Past the grand façade, go over the M25, this time on a bridge, before heading into dense woodland with scattered pines and the chance to spot deer. At the end of the track, just before the gates, turn left and take the track through the forest. As you curve round to the north and the track splits, head right up to the main road, where again take care crossing over to an old concrete milepost.

Inside the forest again, turn left onto the main footpath which meanders through clumps of trees and past the occasional fishpond until you reach Epping Cricket Club again. Take the footpath up to the pitch, keeping to the left of the boundary to rejoin the outward path. Retrace your steps along the common, down into the wood and along the residential streets, before taking the narrow path back down towards Epping Underground Station and the start.

# ⑦ WEST ESSEX

# Snaresbrook to Buckhurst Hill

**Distance** 11km **Time** 3 hours 45
**Terrain** town pavements, forest paths
**Map** OS Explorer 174 **Access** buses to
Snaresbrook from Romford; Central Line
to Snaresbrook Underground Station;
this is a linear walk, returning by Tube

This dense swathe of woodland forming
a green corridor through East London is
part of the extensive Epping Forest area –
2400 hectares of ancient woodland which
stretches for around 24km from Epping
to Forest Gate. The walk also takes in
Queen Elizabeth's Hunting Lodge,
originally built by Henry VIII in 1543 and
then renovated in 1589 for his daughter
Elizabeth to view the hunting of deer
along Chingford Plain.

Start from Snaresbrook Underground
Station and walk down the ramp to the
junction below, where you turn right onto
Hollybush Hill. Soon after, turn left onto
Snaresbrook Road past Eagle Pond, across
which is the Jacobean gothic-style façade
of Snaresbrook Crown Court.

Further along, opposite the car park,
cross over and take the path into the
forest. Keep heading straight and north
until you reach an underpass that leads
you under a roundabout. Bear left
towards Chingford, through another
underpass and then up a mound to the
circular park named the Doughnut. Head
across this and into the trees where you
continue straight on before the path bears
round to the right, over a crossway, and
then loops left alongside the North
Circular Road behind the dense foliage.

Go through another underpass and
then keep left on the track up to a
waymarker, where you walk in the
direction of the lake. This path bears right
and then left before crossing Oak Hill
(a road). Keep straight on, through a
narrow gap and over an unmade track
before entering more woodland. Continue

# Snaresbrook to Buckhurst Hill

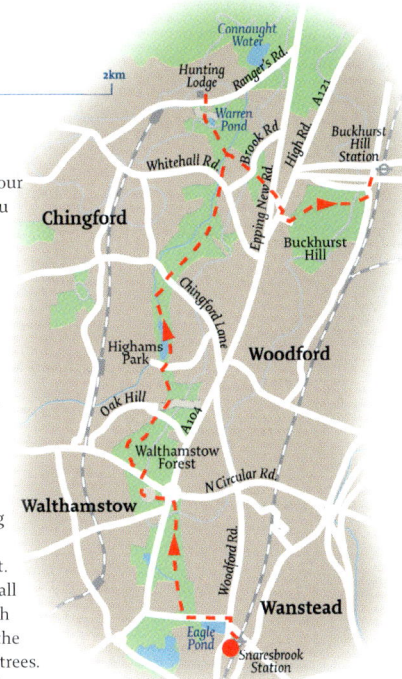

◀ Queen Elizabeth's Hunting Lodge on Chingford Plain

following signs for the lake to emerge at Highams Park and the lake itself. Keeping the water on your left, follow it to the end, where you head left, over a bridge and then diagonally off to your right. This narrow path follows a water-filled ditch before coming out onto a more open path where you bear right. At the crossway, head right again, over another bridge and up to Chingford Lane. Cross over and take the path that leads north towards Whitehall Plain, past sections of a golf course, before coming out onto Whitehall Road.

Now on the plain, carry on along the path in the open, keeping the magnificent oak tree on your right. Just past a hedgerow, there's a small triangular piece of scrub and a path branching left. Take it, cross over the small brook and head up into the trees. At the top, go right past a pond, along a ridged track that leads out onto the road for Queen Elizabeth's Hunting Lodge.

Once you've finished exploring, retrace your steps down to the triangular patch of scrub, where you carry straight on. When you see the road in front, head right towards the 30mph sign, which is where you cross Brook Road into some thick woodland. Follow the path onto an unmade road that comes out onto Epping New Road. Turn right, cross over and then head left down Beech Lane. This bears off to the right to High Road where you turn right and then left down Knighton Lane. At the bottom is a final stretch of woods, where you head left and then right towards the northeast side. The path comes out here onto Forest Edge (a road). Turn left and then right onto Princes Road which gently eases round to the left before straightening up into Victoria Road. A little further along on your right is Buckhurst Hill Underground Station.

# Thorndon Country Park

**Distance** 7km **Time** 2 hours **Terrain** country park tracks, path and lanes **Map** OS Explorer 175 **Access** buses to Brentwood Road, close to the South car park, from Brentwood and Tilbury

South of Brentwood, Thorndon Country Park once formed part of the extensive grounds of Thorndon Hall, designed by Capability Brown and the seat of the Petre family, whose ancestors now reside at Ingatestone Hall. Some features remain, including the hall's imposing entrance gates. Today it is split into North and South parts with woodland, ancient deer parks and traditional meadows for grazing cattle.

Start at the Nature Discovery Centre by the North car park. Constructed from fallen trees from the great storm of 1987, this is the most popular of all Essex Wildlife Trust's visitor centres, regularly attracting 100,000 people a year. Take the path behind the building, heading south past the picnic area, sensory garden and the start of the Gruffalo Trail for little ones. Go straight on past two crossways before the path bears off to the left. At the next corner, head right down into the wooded gully below, before going up and over a bridge onto another path which forms part of the country park's Pebble Walk. Head left and then left again further up, before looping back round on yourself where you carry straight on past the Pebble Wall, an 'ice age wall' showing the geological make-up of this part of the country.

With fencing on your left and a woodland lodge on your right, this path brings you out to Whittington Bars Gate, where you carry straight on. Along this stretch, the modern golf course is on one side, while the ancient grazing meadow is on the other. Eventually, you come to a crossways of paths with a copse of pine

# THORNDON COUNTRY PARK

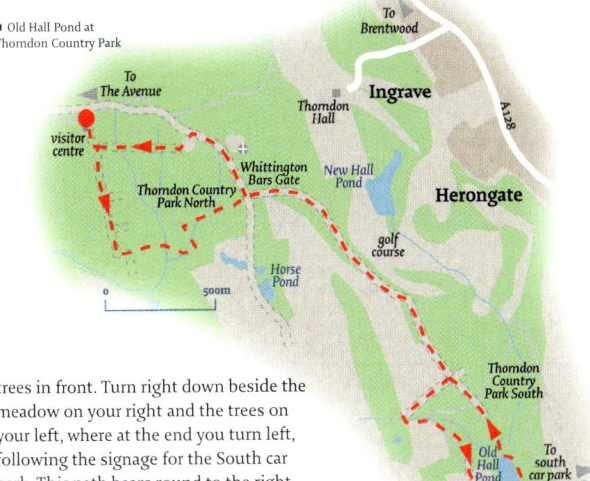

◀ Old Hall Pond at Thorndon Country Park

trees in front. Turn right down beside the meadow on your right and the trees on your left, where at the end you turn left, following the signage for the South car park. This path bears round to the right and up through a gate into another pasture, this time with exquisite views right down towards the Thames Estuary. This is where the Old Hall was built, on your right in the woods, possibly in the 15th century, before being destroyed by fire in the early 18th century. At the bottom of the path, head left and behind the trees you'll discover Old Hall Pond, a lovely stretch of water which would have formed part of the ornamental gardens of the Old Hall. Nestled in amongst the trees, it's positively teeming with wildlife – from dragonflies and butterflies to kingfishers and wildfowl. Walk along the edge and then turn left. At this stage of the walk, if you carried on it would bring you out into the South car park with its Octagon Plantation and further stunning views down to the countryside below.

Back at the pond, continue along the edge where at the end the path narrows greatly. The path now bears left and then when it splits, you need to turn right and climb up the hill to emerge out of the woods – here, the path widens into a gravel track.

After passing the copse of pines, retrace your steps to the Whittington Bars Gate, where this time you head right up the country lane. This goes round to the left past the 'second car park'. Enter the car park and head towards the southwest corner, then take the gate on the right. Beyond this gate, the path goes through the fence to the country park and carries on back to the area behind the Nature Discovery Centre where the walk started.

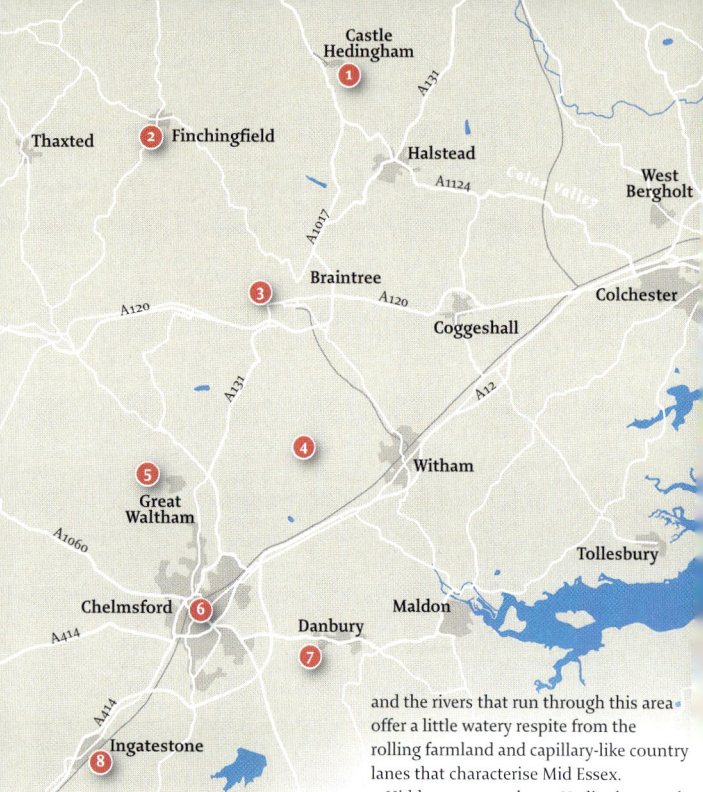

**The heart of Essex** centres around the county town of Chelmsford but is peppered with country villages containing chocolate-box thatched cottages and architecturally divine churches.

Compared to the south and east, there are very few major stretches of water to speak of, although Hanningfield Reservoir and the rivers that run through this area offer a little watery respite from the rolling farmland and capillary-like country lanes that characterise Mid Essex.

Hidden-away castles at Hedingham and Pleshey, as well as country estates at Ingatestone and Terling, hint at the history of land ownership here, while embedded in the larger urban areas of Chelmsford and Braintree is a strong sense of industrial heritage and innovation, as exemplified both by radio inventor Guglielmo Marconi and the silk manufacturing family that made Courtaulds a global name.

Finchingfield Bridge ▶

# Mid Essex

**1 Castle Hedingham** 26
With a fine Norman castle at its heart, this loop takes in some lovely countryside around the historic village

**2 Finchingfield and Great Bardfield** 28
Visit a picturesque village in a bucolic setting which has inspired many notable artists over the years

**3 Braintree** 30
From alleyways to quiet churchyards and industrial estates to old railway lines, this circuit has it all

**4 White Notley to Terling** 32
Head from one pretty village to another along country lanes and through enchanting countryside

**5 Great Waltham to Pleshey** 34
Take in a village built around one of England's most important but sadly long-gone Norman castles

**6 Chelmsford** 36
Tour the handsome county town of Essex, a busy place where the tranquil Rivers Can and Chelmer converge

**7 Danbury** 38
Explore the lanes around a village built on the site of an ancient fort and surrounded by heath and woodlands

**8 Ingatestone** 40
Amble through the fine Essex countryside that envelops this well-heeled town

# Castle Hedingham

**Distance** 6km **Time** 2 hours
**Terrain** village pavements, footpaths (some muddy), country tracks
**Map** OS Explorer 195 **Access** buses to Castle Hedingham from Colchester and Braintree

The village is named after the 'best preserved Norman Keep' in England, Hedingham Castle, which was built in the 12th century by the de Veres, later Earls of Oxford. Now privately owned, the Grade I listed castle can be glimpsed from this route as it weaves through the upper Colne Valley, close to a heritage railway line and past fine farmhouses and chocolate-box thatched cottages.

Start from Nunnery Street, round the corner from the entrance to the castle, and then head up Kirby Hall Road on your right. After 500m, take the footpath on your left, which hugs a field and line of trees before crossing a railway line via gates. This forms part of the Colne Valley Railway, complete with signalbox.

Make sure you close the gates behind you before heading across a meadow, where the route quickly bears left and eventually leads past a small group of trees to Nunnery Street. Turn right, crossing the bridge and then the road, where you'll see a footpath on the left that goes through another gate and follows the river. Keep on this path through a clearing and another gate, where it narrows considerably and gets very boggy, before coming out onto Queen Street. Turn left, cross the road and then the bridge, before taking the footpath on your right which continues alongside the river.

This leads through woodland where, from the embankment at the edge of the field, it is possible to see the tops of the castle battlements complete with flag fluttering in the breeze. Built in around

# CASTLE HEDINGHAM

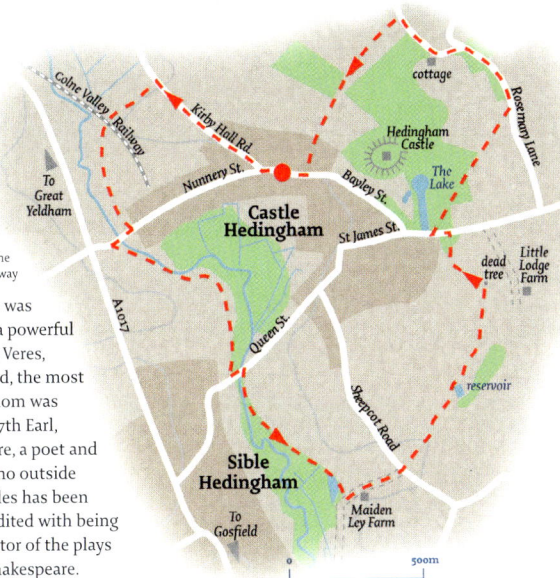

◀ A signalbox on the Colne Valley Railway

1140, the keep was long held by a powerful family, the de Veres, Earls of Oxford, the most famous of whom was perhaps the 17th Earl, Edward de Vere, a poet and playwright who outside academic circles has been popularly credited with being the 'true' creator of the plays by William Shakespeare.

Keeping to the path, cross a wooden bridge and pass a large pond before reaching a farm track where you turn left, past a rather grand old farmhouse. Walk on up the dirt drive to the road, which you cross straight over to the grass verge path ahead. Continue alongside fields and hedgerows until you reach the striking view of a dead tree. Turn left, past the tree and straight across the field to the back of a row of houses, where there are sweeping views down over the Colne Valley. Bear right and at the end of the row, you'll see a footpath heading down through some trees to St James Street, one of the main roads into the village. Cross over to the pavement and then head left down the hill until you come to a footpath on your right, which goes up a steep incline.

As you climb to the top, through the large clumps of pine trees is your best chance of seeing the castle without visiting it. At the end of this path, cross another field to Rosemary Lane, turning left onto this road and continuing to the junction where you bear left to pass a little row of houses and a thatched cottage. A little further on, there's a footpath and gate on your left, which leads down a grassy hill to a narrow footpath at the bottom, through some trees, below some back gardens and eventually back to Nunnery Street.

# Finchingfield and Great Bardfield

**Distance** 8km **Time** 2 hours 30
**Terrain** village pavements, footpaths (some muddy), country tracks
**Map** OS Explorer 195 **Access** buses to Finchingfield from Chelmsford and Braintree

Finchingfield is one of the prettiest villages in the county and lays claim to being 'the most photographed in the country', but Great Bardfield has every bit as much charm as its more popular neighbour. In this glorious part of the Essex countryside, it's no surprise that a community of artists, including Eric Ravilious and Edward Bawden, made their home in Great Bardfield and its surroundings during the middle of the 20th century.

Starting at Finchingfield's picturesque Green, locate the war memorial and head south down Great Bardfield Road from here. After a short distance, turn left down a footpath. At the end, turn right and carry on along a path that is very narrow and muddy in parts as it follows the Finchingfield Brook pretty much all the way.

At a couple of points on this path, you have to divert a little to the right away from the water before returning to carry on ahead once again, crossing a bridge and skirting a field along the way.

At the end of this field, do not take the bridge on your left; go right instead, heading around the field to another bridge on your left, which crosses to a grassy lawn leading to a brick bridge by an old watermill and a pond. Pass the cottage and from the gravel area take the track on your right which quickly morphs into a footpath, going around a gate and then sweeping round to the left by the back gardens of the village of Great Bardfield.

This path skirts around, past one path and bridge on your right, up towards the

◀ Brick House, the home of artist Edward Bawden in Great Bardfield

windmill. Before reaching it, take the path that dives into the darkness by the side of another stream. This bankside path eventually brings you out into Mill Road, where you turn right onto Brook Street and then up the hill into the village's High Street.

Further up, after passing the war memorial, turn right down Bell Lane. As the pavement ends, carry on along the right-hand side for a while before taking the path that leads into a clump of trees and thick hedgerow. At a T-junction of paths, head left over a bridge and then when the path forks keep right as it continues through thick scrub until it gradually brings you out beside a field. Follow the path all the way round, passing the farm, and then head right over another field, up to a gate. Carry straight on here, past the back garden of a cottage and into some more woods, before emerging on top of a grassy hill. Walk down the hill and then, with the corner of Bell Lane visible on your left, turn right onto a track.

As the track nips into another field, carry straight on beside the hedgerow and then into woods, over a bridge and up a ridge where you turn left, go over a stile, and then turn right. This leads you up to a country lane, where you turn left, bringing you to a crossing. Carry straight on here, past some houses to a track on your right. This goes uphill and bears left before gently easing its way past fields and woods. As the track splits, continue straight, on along the grassy rather than the gravel route. This track eventually brings you back to the village of Finchingfield, where you turn left back to the Green.

# Braintree

**Distance** 8km **Time** 2 hours 30
**Terrain** country tracks, footpaths, alleys and pavements **Map** OS Explorer 195
**Access** trains to Braintree from Witham; buses from Colchester and Chelmsford

This walks flits effortlessly from gentle rolling fields and peaceful churchyards to industrial estate roads and winding urban alleyways, taking in a variety of buildings both old and new. It starts along the Flitch Way, the 24km stretch of pathway that was the former Bishop's Stortford to Braintree railway, and ends sneaking down the 'Gants' of the town centre, through the public gardens and past the town hall, both gifted by the Courtauld family who ran their famous silk manufacturing business here.

Start from the railway station where, at the end of the car park, the Flitch Way begins. Carry on along the Flitch Way, under and over bridges but mainly through thick tree-lined cuttings and embankments until you get to the village of Rayne. Just before the first bridge in the village, exit the pathway right and cross the car park to the village hall and recreation ground out towards the road, where you turn right.

At the crossroads, go straight on. A short distance further along on your right, take the track up to All Saints Church, its ornate Tudor West Tower adorned with stepped buttresses and an octagonal stair turret. Head to the southeast corner of the churchyard to pick up the footpath that intersects the fields ahead. At the end, in front, cross the metal footbridge and then immediately head right into the hedgerow over a wooden bridge. This path bears round to the left and rises to eventually reach a metal kissing gate leading into a field.

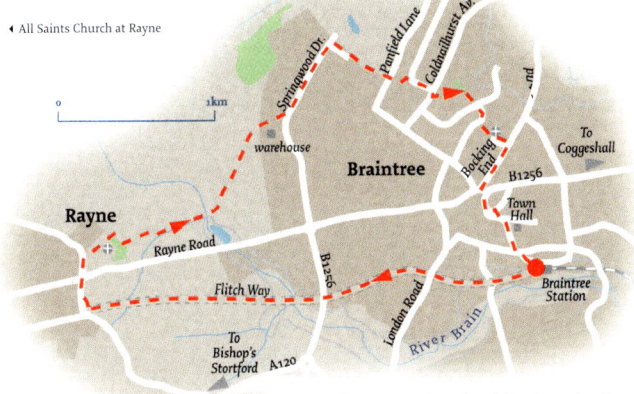

◀ All Saints Church at Rayne

Keep left, go through a further gate and then another one at the end of the field, which gives access to a small wooded area around a large warehouse.

At the far end of this building, you come out onto Springwood Drive where you head left alongside a series of business units. Beyond Finch Drive, take the narrow path on the right which leads into a cyclepath and then onto Panfield Lane. Go straight across this onto another path. This will bring you out to Lancaster Way by the entrance of a primary school, where you turn right. Head down to Coldnailhurst Avenue, where you cross to your right, behind a bus stop, to a stretch of open land.

Take the left diagonal path down to a large area of scrubland where you'll find a crossing of paths. Turn right to go up and then across into Rosemary Avenue, which bears round to the right. Just after it straightens out, there's another alleyway on your left. Take that and zigzag around to emerge by St Peter's Church. Go around the church and ahead you'll see the corner entrance to the town's public gardens. Keep straight on, past the delightful late Victorian Keepers' Cottage, now a café, and turn right onto a path that leads to the entrance at the corner of Bocking End. Go up the hill into the town centre, crossing over into the little square of Bank Street. Carry straight on between the shops and down one of the narrow alleyways, or 'Gants', that are dotted all around Braintree's town centre. This brings you out into a row of shops where you turn left, then right and down into Market Place. Cross over at the town hall and then head down to South Street, where you go left and then immediately right down Station Approach to the start of the walk.

# White Notley to Terling

Distance 13km Time 4 hours
Terrain village pavements, footpaths, country tracks and lanes
Map OS Explorer 183 Access buses and trains to White Notley from Braintree and Witham

Following stretches of the Essex Way, this walk weaves its way to Terling, a pretty village with a number of fabulous claims to fame. Perhaps the best is Terling Place, residence of the Lords of Rayleigh, a family of agricultural pioneers and acclaimed scientists, including the Nobel Prize-winning physicist who discovered argon. Terling Windmill, meanwhile, featured in the 1930s film *Oh, Mr Porter!*

Start from Vicarage Avenue, a short walk from the station and bus stops on the main road. Opposite the school entrance, take the footpath that leads out to a track. Turn left and then immediately right, taking the path just above the track which leads down to the back of a cottage, where you turn right. Now on the Essex Way, carry on to the main road, where you turn left, take care crossing over and then head right down another farm track. Eventually, the track leads round to the right and then at a metal gate heads left before winding its way down to the country lane. Turn left onto this.

The lane gently sweeps around some picturesque countryside to reach the village of Terling. At the main junction, cross over into Crow Pond Road. At the next crossing, keep left and then curve around past the gates of Terling Place to a common, where All Saints Church is on your left and a handsome Georgian chapel is on your right. Continue along Church

# WHITE NOTLEY TO TERLING

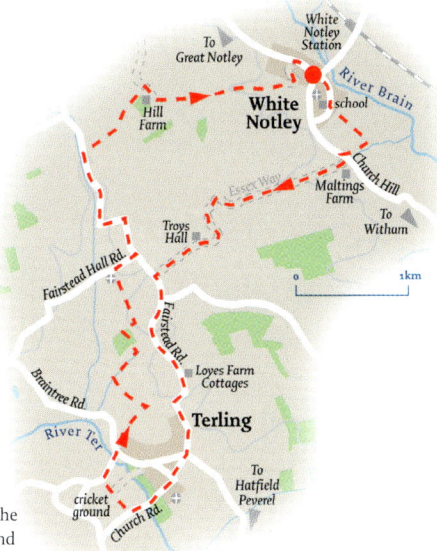

◀ The Essex Way towards Terling

Road, down the hill and through a wood. After leaving the wood and continuing, take a footpath on your right which goes over a stile and then past the village cricket pitch. At the gate and track, carry straight on up to Norman Hill, where you turn right to walk down to the ford over the River Ter. Cross the bridge and head up to the T-junction, where you turn left and then immediately go right up another track on the Essex Way.

Follow the path up and then, rather than carrying straight on, go down round to the left alongside the meadow to the bottom, where you head over to the right towards the woods. The path slips through the trees before coming out into a field where you turn right. After 50m, the path bears left across the field towards Fairstead Church in the distance. Go through the churchyard and onto the country lane, then right down to the crossing and turn left.

Listen out for traffic as you walk along the lane and take care as it leads sharp left and then right. After a long stretch of road, there's a footpath on your right which takes you up the side of a field, turns right and then goes up through a gap on the left before continuing up to a line of trees, behind which there's a wide gravel area. Turn right and then after a few metres go left down a track that eventually narrows between two lines of trees as it reaches a gravel driveway track. This then sweeps around an impressive collection of houses and converted barns before heading right down to White Notley's high street. Turn right and walk down the busy road to the crossing of Station Road and Vicarage Avenue, where you walk back up to the start.

# Great Waltham to Pleshey

**Distance** 9km **Time** 2 hours 30
**Terrain** footpaths, village roads, country tracks **Map** OS Explorer 183
**Access** buses to Great Waltham from Chelmsford and Braintree

This walk connects the two attractive villages of Great Waltham and Pleshey, the latter perhaps most famous for one of the most important castles of the early medieval period, even getting a mention in Shakespeare's *Richard II*. Now just a mound, a moat and a bridge, you can only catch glimpses from the footpath. Great Waltham has its own interesting heritage with an Elizabethan Guildhall and a handsome country house. The first English woman executed under the Witchcraft Act of 1563 came from here.

Start from South Street and walk up to the junction where you go right down Chelmsford Road. Pass the Elizabethan Guildhall on your left and carry on until you reach a lodge house with the inscription *Esse Quam Videri* ('To Be, Rather Than to Seem To Be'), the family motto of the Tuffnells who lived in Langleys at the end of the driveway. The driveway is also a footpath, so you can see Langleys for yourself further along it on your right.

Carry straight on through the beautiful parkland, still grazed by cattle, to another lodge, where you cross the main road to the field opposite.

Keep straight on until the path leads into another field, where you turn right. This is part of the Essex Way, the longest of the county's long-distance paths. At the end of this field, cross the road and then head up a bank which circles a fishing lake. Follow the water around to the right to the far end. From here, head left onto another path which hugs a line of trees to its right. As the path winds round to the

# GREAT WALTHAM TO PLESHEY

◀ Pleshey Mount View Point community garden

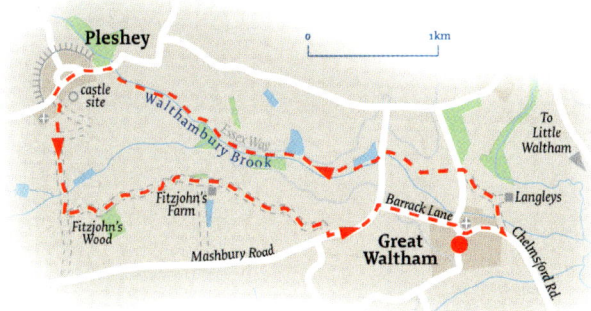

right, there's another lake, almost hidden by the hedgerow, which you bypass. At the end of this, the path sweeps round to the left – just before a large concrete slab, go right.

With Walthambury Brook to your left and fields on your right, the path gently meanders westwards until the trees end and the path skips over into the next field, while still continuing straight. As the path ends, it narrows between a thicket of trees and bushes and the metal fence to a pump station. Out on the main country lane, bear left into the ridiculously pretty village of Pleshey, home to what was once one of the most important castles in England. Now hidden away behind thatched cottages, neat brick walls and quite a lot of trees and bushes, the privately owned motte and bailey is closed to the general public.

As you head up and around The Street, you can get a glimpse of the 15th-century arched bridge that crosses the castle moat by a back gate on your left, just after Back Lane. A little further up, turn left down Pump Lane and, 100m up the track, there's a small stretch of grass leading to a padlocked gate, with the remains of the castle beyond.

Opposite the gate, there's a path that leads onto a concrete farm track. Walk down this and then up again until you join a bridleway on your left. This atmospheric track winds eastwards through arboreal arches and past a couple of houses and thick hedgerows before arriving at Mashbury Road, where you turn left. This road doesn't have a path, so take care of traffic, but after looping right into Barrack Lane, it brings you back into Great Waltham. At the T-junction with the church in front, go right and then after the corner head right again up South Street to the start.

# Chelmsford

**Distance** 4km **Time** 1 hour
**Terrain** city centre pavements, riverside paths and bridges **Map** OS Explorer 183
**Access** Chelmsford is well served by buses and trains

Chelmsford is the county town of Essex and more impressively the home of radio. Guglielmo Marconi opened the world's first 'radio' factory here in 1899 and in 1920 made the first official public sound broadcast with opera star Nellie Melba. This walk gently glides over the city's numerous bridges, trading the everyday hustle of shoppers and commuters for the peaceful banks of its two rivers.

Start from the railway station, crossing over to Park Road. With the pub on your left, head through the small crescent with the racks of commuter bikes and then between buildings either side to emerge in an open space, where you walk diagonally down to your right to the main road. Head through the colourfully graffiti-lined subway which brings you out into the city's attractive park. Carry on along the path that hugs the lake to your right until you get to the 'roundabout' of paths, where you bear right. Before the striking railway viaduct, cross the bridge on your left, after which you turn left and double back on yourself on the opposite side of the River Can. At the T-junction, turn left again and go over the bridge back into the park.

Turn right here and continue along the path, which eventually brings you parallel with the back of Essex County Cricket Ground across the water. Walk under the city bypass, keeping right as you go through Bell Meadow. At the end, cross New London Road to your right and carry

◀ Chelmsford's Georgian Shire Hall

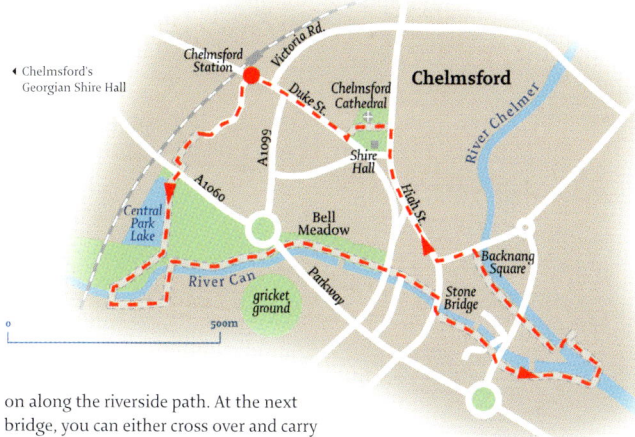

on along the riverside path. At the next bridge, you can either cross over and carry on by the river on the other side or continue straight on, but if you do stay on the left-hand side you'll need to cross over at the next bridge. This is Stone Bridge: from here, if you go right down Moulsham Street and then across the bypass, you'll find Hall Street where, in 1899, the Marconi Wireless Radio Factory was established.

Back by the river on the south side, King's Head Walk winds its way under more bridges and alongside a car park while still offering up lovely views of the riverbank. As the path continues, you'll see the confluence of the River Can with the River Chelmer over to your left. At the next bridge, cross and then turn left to now double back on yourself before turning left again to cross the Chelmer via another bridge.

Turn right and you're now on French's Walk, this time alongside the Chelmer. Past the poles of the city's canoe club, this brings you into the heart of the 'shopping' district, where at Backnang Square, named after the city's German twin town, you turn left.

Carry on into the pedestrianised High Street, where you turn right and head on up to the city's Shire Hall with its Georgian façade. Keep right into New Street where, after around 200m, you go left up into the churchyard of Chelmsford Cathedral. Originally the town's parish church, it became a cathedral in 1914 with the creation of the Chelmsford diocese.

Walk south through the narrow alley that leads into Duke Street before turning right and heading back up to the railway station, crossing over at the junction with Victoria Road.

# Danbury

**Distance** 6km **Time** 2 hours
**Terrain** country park tracks, country lanes, footpaths **Map** OS Explorer 183
**Access** buses to Danbury from Chelmsford and Southend

While 112m above sea level might not sound particularly lofty, Danbury is, in fact, one of the high points of the county. The village is built on the site of an early Iron Age fort and was aptly the inspiration for the fictional village of Danebury in the BBC series, *The Detectorists*. This walk takes in the pretty 'lanes' that intersect the area south of the main village between its two green spaces, Danbury Country Park and the National Trust-run Danbury Common.

Start the walk from the Danbury Common National Trust car park, just a short way from the bus stop on the main Bicknacre Road. Opposite the main information board, there's a narrow path that leads back to the road. Take care crossing over and carry on down the first of the stony 'lanes', Plumptree Lane. At the end, take the footpath almost straight ahead that runs through the woods in typically meandering fashion until it comes out on Sporehams Lane. Carry straight on and, just before it winds round to the left, go right up Fitzwalter Lane. Halfway up, take the lower left-hand of two parallel tracks which leads off to a line of smart houses. At the end of the houses, you'll find a footpath that nips through some woods at the edge of a field, with occasional glimpses of the tree-lined fields that roll below.

This path brings you out onto Woodhill Road – take care crossing to the back of

◀ Danbury Common

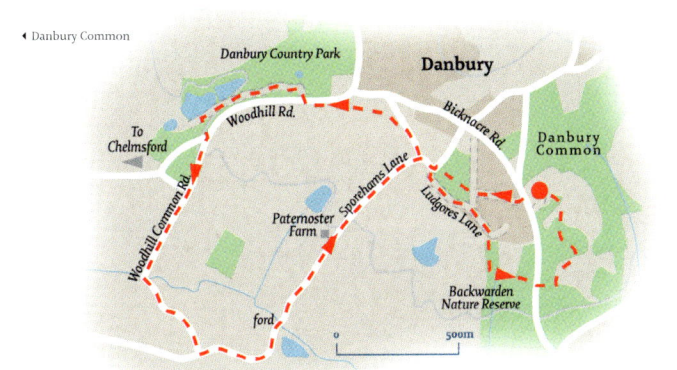

Danbury Country Park's Woods car park via the unsigned exit. Walk on through to the park's entrance where you keep left round to the park's Lakes car park. Both of these car parks are good starting points for exploring the former medieval deer park further.

Again, walk straight across this car park before going past some lakes on your right to a toilet block and gate, where you turn left down a footpath. This takes you up a steep ridge to the edge of the main road. Take care crossing to Woodhill Common Road, which drops gently down into the valley before rising up again to a T-junction. Head left here to follow the lane as it swings back round and down past a ford before gradually climbing back up to the village. It's not exactly the north face of the Eiger, but in Essex this is a nice little incline to get the calves working.

At the top, you'll find yourself back where you crossed earlier. Go back round to the woods but this time head right and around into Ludgores Lane. At the end, go right down a footpath that leads into Backwarden Nature Reserve. At the first opportunity, turn left and cross the nature reserve to the track that leads out onto Bicknacre Road. Take care crossing and carry on to the common. Danbury Common is the second largest tract of commonland in the county and is a Site of Special Scientific Interest (SSSI). During the Napoleonic Wars, because of its elevation, it was used as a strategic defence in the event of invasion.

Ignore the paths edging their way alongside the road to your left and right and continue straight on. After about 100m, a wider path goes off to the left – take this and carry on in this general northerly direction, either through the woods or along the heather- and gorse-scattered common to return to the car park at the start.

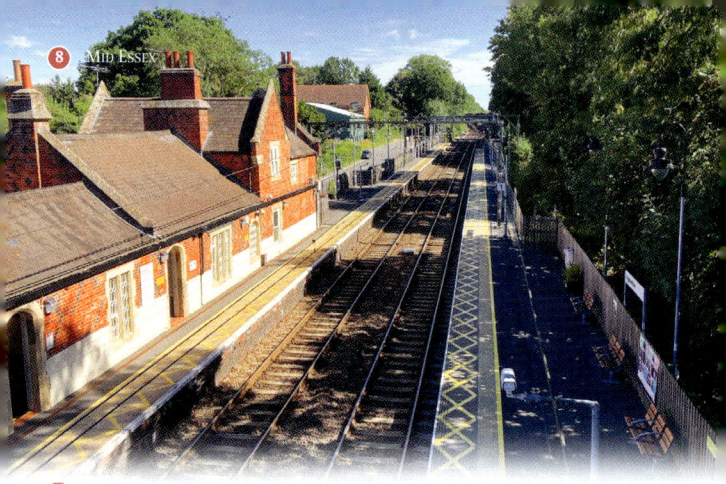

# Ingatestone

**Distance** 5km **Time** 1 hour 30
**Terrain** footpaths, field tracks, country lanes **Map** OS Explorer 175 **Access** buses to Ingatestone from Chelmsford and Brentwood; trains to Ingatestone from London Liverpool Street and Chelmsford

While this is most definitely commuter-belt country, within minutes you can be in the heart of the Essex countryside with its weather-boarded churches, rolling hills and some of the most stunning country homes in England. Among them is Ingatestone Hall, open to the public on a Sunday and Wednesday between Easter and September. This walk is still worth an outing at any time for St Mary's Church and the pretty Victorian ticket hall at the station.

Start from Ingatestone Station which, despite being on the London to Norwich Mainline, is reminiscent of the *Railway Children* with its Tudor style and decorative brickwork. Take the path which, if you have your back to the ticket office, is diagonally to the right.

Initially running behind a fence, it cuts in to the left and then goes through stands of trees either side before leading up to the village's cricket pitch and recreation ground. After crossing a driveway, keep left along the green space towards the church, where you head right just before the playpark. Walk towards the park's little lake, before cutting across the skateboard area to the footpath behind. Over the railway bridge, keep right on the wide path that runs between two fields.

This eventually brings you to a line of chestnut and oak trees where, towards the end, you head left behind a group of farm buildings and then the back of Ingatestone Hall. Keep to the path as it goes down alongside another field to a

*Ingatestone's Victorian railway station*

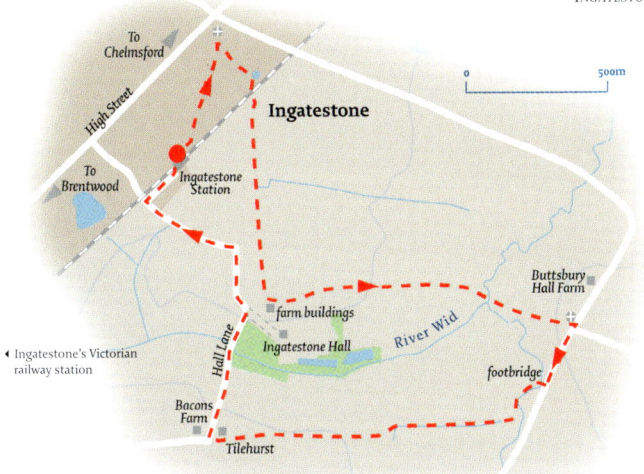

footbridge which crosses the River Wid at the bottom. Cross this, ignoring the footbridge to your right.

After the river, walk up to the church at the top of the hill. This is St Mary's at Buttsbury, the north door of which is believed to be Saxon in origin while the rest is 14th and 15th century. There's a rather nice story about St Botolph preaching under a pear tree on the site in the 7th century and to commemorate this another such tree has been planted in the churchyard.

From the church, turn right to walk down the country lane, where soon there's another footbridge on your right. After crossing, bear left and keep left alongside a ditch to follow the right of way across fields, with Ingatestone Hall to your right behind a line of trees.

Continue onto a tree-lined track, emerging on Hall Lane past the magnificent red-brick Tilehurst House, built in 1884 with soaring chimneys and a tower with a belvedere.

Keeping an eye out for traffic, turn right and head along the lane, passing the entrance to Ingatestone Hall soon after you have crossed a bridge. The hall has been home to the Petre family since Henry VIII's time, when Sir William was secretary of state to the monarch. When open, check out the 18th-century gatehouse with its striking clock turret, among many other architectural delights.

Continue along the lane as it climbs around to the right before it sweeps back round to the left. As you come back into the village, just before the level crossing, turn right into the cycle park and disabled car park. At the end, head onto the platform and cross the bridge to the start.

Cobbled street in Old Leigh leading to the marshes ▶

**George Orwell described Essex** as 'the Kingdom between London and the Sea', and nowhere is this more apposite than in the area covered by the routes in this chapter, which show the watery 'kingdom' of the Thames Estuary in all its glory.

Industry and nature go hand in hand as the estuary unfurls east from Rainham to Southend. From cranes shifting shipping containers onto docks to the high-pitched trill of reversing trucks, the whole area pulses with industrial energy.

Forts form part of the backdrop too, as protection against the threat of foreign invaders, as well as huge sea walls defending this vulnerable part of the country against more natural threats.

Further along the 'coast' at Southend, entertainment is the order of the day with amusements, a theme park and the world's longest pleasure pier. And at Hadleigh, there's the chance to catch mountain bikers zipping along dusty ravines and hurling themselves over jumps on the Mountain Bike Course created for the London 2012 Olympics.

42

# South Essex

**1** **Rainham to Purfleet** 44
With London's skyscrapers at your back, take a walk on the wild side along the tidal Thames Estuary

**2** **Tilbury Fort and Docks** 46
Unsurprisingly for what was once London's main port, there's poignant history as well as industry found here

**3** **East Tilbury and Coalhouse Fort** 48
Having guarded the Thames from raiders and invaders for centuries, this is an unmissable spot for history fans

**4** **Fobbing** 50
Pause to reflect on the beginnings of the Peasants' Revolt before continuing through rough grassland and saltmarsh

**5** **Plotlands and Basildon** 52
Take a tour of some delightful nature reserves not far from one of Essex's most built-up areas

**6** **Canvey Island** 54
Leave the holiday chalets and cafés behind and follow the sea wall for extensive coast and creek views

**7** **Hadleigh** 56
Loop around a 13th-century castle and enjoy great estuary views, then look out for mountain bikers on the return

**8** **Leigh to Southend** 58
Go from a charming old fishing port to a popular seaside town along a glorious stretch of coastline

# Rainham to Purfleet

**Distance** 8km **Time** 2 hours 30
**Terrain** town pavements, cyclepath and sea wall **Map** OS Explorer 162
**Access** trains to Rainham from Southend and London Fenchurch Street; this is a linear walk, returning to the start by train

Rainham Marshes form an archetypal tract of wild land right in the heart of an ever growing industrial urban landscape. It could have been a very different place, with plans for a huge theme park shelved in the 1990s and then the Ministry of Defence temporarily using it as a firing range until 2006 when it became a protected nature reserve. Now it provides a glorious natural contrast to the bustle of the Thames Estuary.

Start the walk from Rainham Station, where you head behind the ticket office to the footbridge which goes over the railway line and down a ramp onto a cyclepath below. This path fleetingly intersects the large expanse of greenbelt that makes up Rainham Marshes before coming out onto a roundabout. Briefly head left to go under the A13 dual carriageway, using the pedestrian crossings by the slipways, before heading across to the continuation of the cyclepath which very helpfully offers up distance markers to your eventual destination of Purfleet.

Largely enclosed by reedbeds, this wide path winds its way around, past marsh ditches, bundles of hedgerow and ponds teeming with wildlife, until it eventually comes out on Coldharbour Lane. Cross over, head left and after a few metres turn right to follow the long narrow driveway which loops round to the left up to Riverside car park. Just before you reach the car park, there's a gap on your right which leads down to a long jetty, beside which a number of concrete barges have settled into the thick Thames Estuary

◀ Signpost along the Thames Path

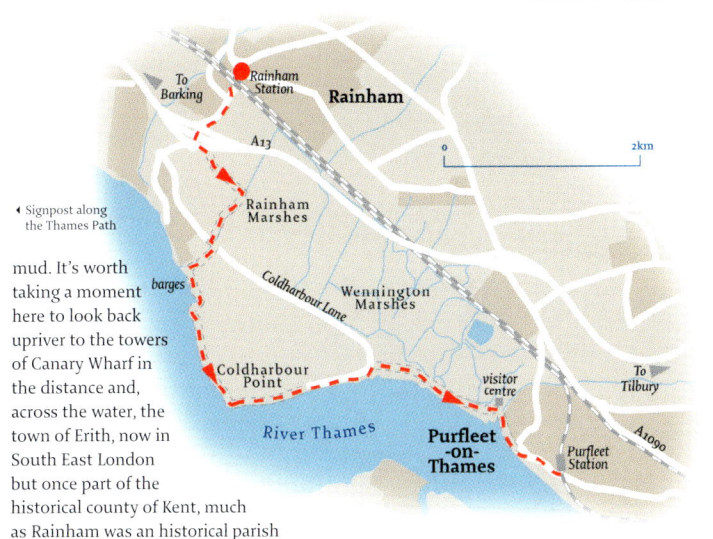

mud. It's worth taking a moment here to look back upriver to the towers of Canary Wharf in the distance and, across the water, the town of Erith, now in South East London but once part of the historical county of Kent, much as Rainham was an historical parish of Essex.

There is some conjecture about how the concrete barges came about but it seems they were built during the Second World War to aid the Normandy Landings and then sunk in the estuary to protect the flood defences after the tidal surge of 1953, which devastated the entire length of the Essex coastline from Harwich right the way around to Coldharbour. Also, look out for John Kaufman's playful *Diver* sculpture which, depending on the tide, can be seen in various states of exposure.

From this point, the path to Purfleet is very clear as it weaves its way round the Erith Rands, mirroring the direction of the Thames as it loops downstream towards Dartford and the majestic sight of the Queen Elizabeth II Bridge in the distance.

Before that, nature swaps places with industry at various points, in particular at the Rainham Landfill Site which processes 1.5 million tonnes of waste each year, producing enough electricity to power 14,600 homes from the methane gas that the waste creates.

As you make your way towards Purfleet, you pass the hides and paths of the RSPB Reserve, as well as its award-winning multi-hued visitor centre. Pass the centre, cross the bridge and continue along the riverfront path until you reach Purfleet's Heritage and Military Centre, housed in an old gunpowder magazine. At the green just beyond this, head up to the road and turn right. Cross over the roundabout and, 100m further down, the railway station is on your left.

# Tilbury Fort and Docks

**Distance** 4km **Time** 1 hour
**Terrain** sea wall, footpaths, town pavements, cyclepaths
**Map** OS Explorer 163 **Access** trains to Tilbury from Southend and London Fenchurch Street; buses to Gravesend Ferry Terminal from Basildon and Grays

It's fairly obvious as you do this walk that Tilbury is a vibrant working town that pulsates with industry. But you don't have to look far to find a wealth of history dating back centuries. This includes 'England's most spectacular' late 17th-century fort, the site of the World's End pub mentioned in Samuel Pepys' diary and London's principal port, built in 1886, where the *Empire Windrush* made its symbolic landing in 1948.

Start from the fort's Water Gate, a spectacular stone façade complete with ornately carved depictions of classical and 17th-century weapons. Just outside, head up the steps past a large granite rock, which was taken from Culloden Moor, the site of the famous battle in 1746. It remembers the Scottish prisoners from the battle who either died on the Thames prison ships or within the fort.

Up on the reinforced sea wall, head east along the concrete walkaway past the inner moat and then the outer ditch, which formed part of the fort's extensive defences. As it winds round a grazing meadow past the Bill Meroy Creek, named after an 18th-century cattle farmer, there's a set of steps on your right. If you go over these steps and follow the estuary path, you can continue on the Two Forts Way to reach Coalhouse Fort after 5km.

For this walk, however, head left and follow the path alongside the creek to a kissing gate, where you go left on a raised path parallel to the track below. At the

◀ The Water Gate at Tilbury Fort

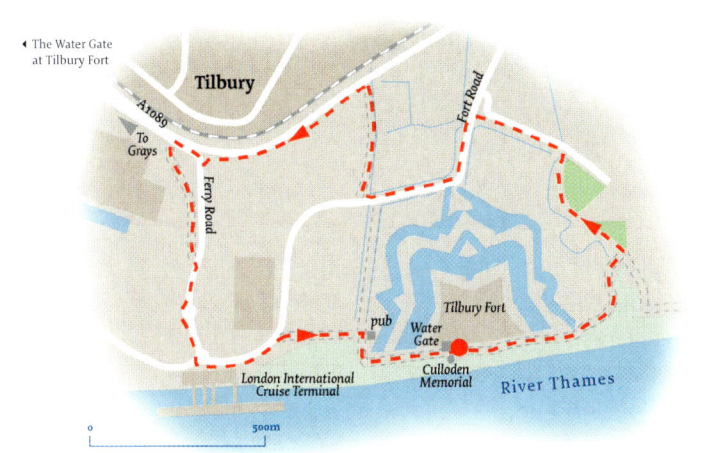

end, turn left onto Fort Road; it is usually quiet but care should still be taken.

Just before the cattle grid ahead, take the cyclepath on your left but carry straight on rather than going left back down to the river. After a few metres, cross Fort Road and continue along the cyclepath that leads round to the main A1089, where you head left. When you reach the road that goes down to the London International Cruise Terminal, cross this to find another cyclepath heading off to your left after around 50m. This brings you out to a couple of roundabouts on Ferry Road where ahead you will see the terminal building. Originally built in the 1930s but more recently refurbished, it was where the 'Ten Pound Poms' headed off for a new life in Australia after the Second World War and where more than 800 West Indians on board the *HMT Empire Windrush* landed in 1948 looking for a new life in the UK.

Head around to the vehicle bridge that leads down to the Gravesend Ferry Terminal and, off to your right, take a walk down the covered walkway which has a fascinating interactive art installation celebrating the memories of those who came over as part of the Windrush Generation.

Returning to Fort Road, head right and then up to the sea wall, which carries on east towards The World's End pub, site of a tavern since the 17th century. It was once the site of the terminal for the Tilbury to Gravesend Ferry and a very popular agricultural market.

Carry on walking along the sea wall, past the grassy mounds below that once housed the fort's magazines, to return to the Water Gate at the start.

# East Tilbury and Coalhouse Fort

**Distance** 8.5km **Time** 2 hours 30
**Terrain** sea wall, footpaths, town pavements, roads **Map** OS Explorer 163
**Access** buses to East Tilbury from Grays and Basildon; trains to East Tilbury from Southend and London Fenchurch Street

Thanks to its position on the Thames Estuary, East Tilbury has been vital to the nation's sea defences for centuries. The first earth rampart and towers were constructed in the 1400s with Henry VIII ordering an artillery blockhouse to be built here in 1539. The current fort dates back to the 1860s but fell into disrepair after being decommissioned following the Second World War.

Start the walk from the fort's visitor information centre, which tells the history of Coalhouse from its early days right up to modern times when it was used in the opening scenes of the 2005 movie, *Batman Begins*. While the building itself is inaccessible, the surrounding public park has plenty of sights to take in.

Facing the block, head round to the right and do a loop of the fort, past the moated lakes to the large pillbox that looks very much like it might be a modern art installation. Just past this old minefield control tower, turn right and head for the sea wall which forms part of the England Coast Path.

Carry on along this concrete structure, with the actual wall on your left as it continues north along the Thames Estuary with wonderful views of the Kent coastline across the water.

Nearing the end of the wall, with the London Gateway Port off to your right, go over a sluice and then, as the sea wall ends, head up onto the grassy bank and

## EAST TILBURY AND COALHOUSE FORT

◀ The old entrance at Coalhouse Fort

then go left inland and down to a path that leads into a dense clump of trees and bushes. This narrow path mainly bears west as it winds its way between the high fence of a nature reserve on your right and a marsh ditch and woodland on your left.

With the path bearing in a more northerly direction, you come to a metal kissing gate on your right which leads back to the England Coast Path, but you need to turn left and carry on towards East Tilbury Station. Before you get there, follow a grassy strip of land next to the recreation ground to the main road. Over the road, to the left, there's a driveway with bollards leading into a new-build housing estate. Follow this and then, with the railway line tight on your right, keep going. Where the houses end, carry on past some trees and into a field, still following the railway line to reach a crossing. Instead of going over the railway, head left alongside the field and a line of thick hedgerow.

Over on your left is the derelict Bata shoe factory. It was built in 1932 and formed part of an industrial estate called 'Bata-Ville' that also included shops, sports facilities, a theatre and workers' homes set in landscaped gardens. The modernist factory is all that remains after the estate was shut down in 2005.

As the hedgerow thins out, carry on along the grassy path towards the trees. Here, the path sinks into an enclosed line of trees and hedges until it reaches the country road at the end where you turn left. Almost immediately you then keep right down Station Road, which has no path but stretches of verge that you can dip into when traffic passes.

At the end of the road, turn right and head on down into East Tilbury village, past the church on your left and back to the fort.

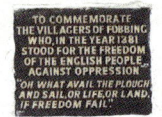

# Fobbing

**Distance** 8.5km **Time** 2 hours 30
**Terrain** footpaths (some very uneven), tracks, town pavements
**Map** OS Explorer 175 **Access** buses to Fobbing from Basildon and Grays

There's quite a claim on the sign outside the village pub – that Fobbing is the 'Cradle of Democracy' – but there's no doubting the village's involvement with the Peasants' Revolt of 1381, which began with riots in several Essex villages and eventually led to the march on London. This walk takes in the plaque to those who 'stood for the freedom of the English People', before heading out onto the marshes where industry merges seamlessly with nature.

Start from outside St Michael's Church and make your way back to the main road where you need to turn left down Lion Hill, cross over and go past the pub where the revolutionaries are commemorated.

Carry on along this road as it climbs back up the hill and into the outskirts of Corringham. Pass the church, cross over and turn left down Herd Lane, following it to the end to pick up an unmade track that heads off left. As it opens up, you get your first view of the London Gateway Port off to your right. Carry straight on and take the footpath ahead that goes downhill before bearing left into the woods. Follow this path past private fishing lakes and as you cross a metal-railed bridge, take the stile on your right. This path takes you through an open patch of land surrounded by trees and hedgerows, before coming to another stile, over which you turn right. A few metres down this path, there's a gate in front and large pylon above. Take the path on your left, which heads out towards the marshes on a narrow ridge, which at various points is very uneven with large crevices. Over another couple of fairly

◀ Plaque at the White Lion

rickety stiles, at the footpath signpost carry straight on. This grazing marsh still has cattle on it, so beware if you're taking dogs with you.

It gets a bit tricky to follow the actual footpath here, what with the grass mounds, cattle tracks and bramble bushes, so keep in mind you're heading east towards a concrete bunker-type structure which looks a little like a very fat bridge: this is the Fobbing Horse Flood Barrier, built in the 1970s as part of the defences for Canvey Island.

As you get to a reedbed, follow it around to a stile, which brings you up to the sea wall by Fobbing Creek. Head right around to the Fobbing Horse Flood Barrier. Just south of the barrier, there's another footpath marker sending you back to the grazing marsh. At the end of the path, turn right and continue until you see a couple of metal gates off to your left. Go over both of the stiles and then turn left.

Follow this path as it bears right, edging alongside a ditch and fence. At the footpath marker, keep straight on. Again, the path is difficult to follow, but try to keep between the hedgerows, this time aiming for the tower of St Michael's Church in Fobbing in the distance.

Eventually, this brings you back to the footpath marker and the ridged path that you came in on. Retrace your steps to the gate and pylon. Here, turn right and then continue straight on along a rather ornamental path that feels a little like you're going down to the bottom of a garden. This winds round to the bottom of Wharf Road, where you turn left and then head up the hill back to the church and the start of the walk.

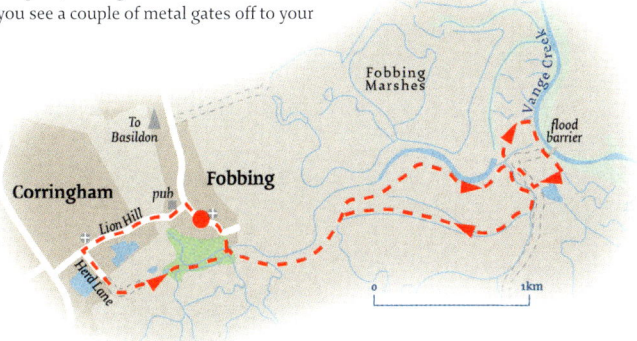

# Plotlands and Basildon

**Distance** 13km **Time** 4 hours
**Terrain** woodland paths, country tracks, footpaths (some muddy), town pavements **Map** OS Explorer 175
**Access** no public transport to the start

On this walk, you're never far away from one of the largest urban areas within the county and yet, at times, all you can hear is birdsong. That's because this corner of Basildon New Town has not one but four nature reserves to explore. Starting at Langdon Nature Discovery Park, run by Essex Wildlife Trust and part of the old Plotlands site where London families snapped up cheap 'plots' of land in the 1930s, this walk can be broken down into smaller loops if you prefer.

From the Nature Discovery Centre car park, walk up the hill into the nature reserve itself, passing the Haven, the last remaining Plotlands house in England. Keep on the path with the fields on your right until you reach an open fenced entrance to the woods with a yellow waymarker. This path takes you up and through the woods, eventually bearing round to the right. Carry on past a pond and ignore a stile which leads into a field on your right; instead, continue through the woods, heading left and up a steep hill until you come to a clearing just before the road with a mobile phone mast in the distance.

Take care crossing the main road towards the entrance of the Westley Heights Country Park. Follow the drive which leads through the park's car park and fork left just after *The Woodsman* sculpture. Stay on the wide track that winds all the way round the park, almost returning full circle. By a field, you'll see a

# PLOTLANDS AND BASILDON

◀ The Haven, the last of the Plotlands houses

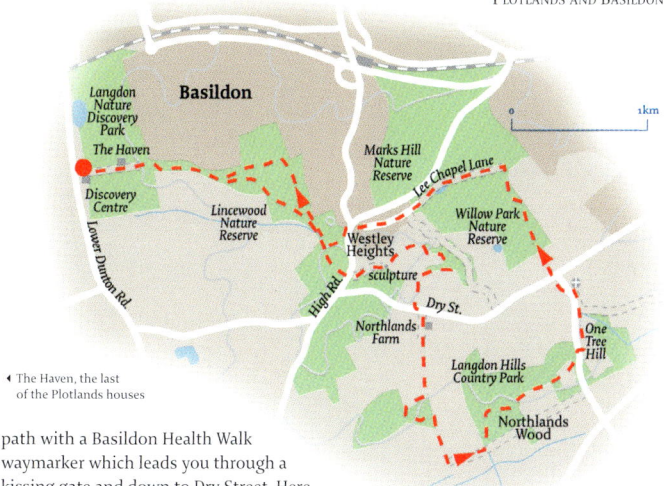

path with a Basildon Health Walk waymarker which leads you through a kissing gate and down to Dry Street. Here, turn left and then bear right into Northlands Farm. Past the farm's outbuildings, head down into the fields, where you can see the Thames Estuary spread out in front of you.

Look out for the footpath to your right, which you take and then almost immediately fork left into another field. Skirt around the meadow until you reach a kissing gate that leads into woods. Turn left after going through this and then keep on this path until you come out into the open onto a bridleway. This leads back towards the estuary, before bearing left towards Northlands Wood. At the map, go through the gate and climb up through the woods in a northeasterly direction until you reach One Tree Hill car park.

Cross the road and turn left down the hill, then up again to a gravel path, where you turn left. This brings you out at the Memorial Church. Cross the road and continue on the path over Dry Street and into Willow Park Nature Reserve.

Carry on for about 1km where, at a crosspaths, you turn left. This is another long stretch that eventually leads out of the woods and into a quiet residential area on Lee Chapel Lane. Stay on this until it reaches High Road, where you cross over and turn left. Past the bus stop, take the footpath on your right, which brings you back into the woods. At the end, turn right and head downhill: you may recognise this section from earlier in the walk. Rather than retrace your steps, stay on the wider path until you see a lamppost by another crosspaths, where you turn left. This path, after a few zigzags, leads you back down to Langdon Nature Discovery Centre at the start.

# Canvey Island

**Distance** 6km **Time** 2 hours
**Terrain** sea wall, unmade tracks, town pavements **Map** OS Explorer 175
**Access** buses to Canvey Island from Basildon and Southend

Canvey is the county's most populated island, with around 40,000 inhabitants. Lying just above sea level, it is prone to flooding – most tragically in the Great Flood of 1953, when 58 islanders lost their lives – and this threat still dominates island life today. The island's defensive sea wall offers panoramic views across to the Kent coastline, as well as Hadleigh, Benfleet and Southend. In the event of any renewal work to the southern shoreline defences, the wall can be bypassed just inland or, at low tides, via the beachfront.

Start from Canvey's iconic building, the art deco Labworth Beach Café, originally built in 1933 and designed by Ove Arup who was involved in the design of the Sydney Opera House. It formed part of a building boom on the island when Canvey became the fastest growing seaside resort in the country.

Head east along the sea wall or the beach itself if the tide is out. This is Concord Beach with its tidal paddling pools and colourful murals painted along the wall, showcasing community groups and clubs, as well as some of the island's history, including the flood of 1953.

Head around the sea wall to the Island Yacht Club on Point Road. Just beyond the clubhouse, between some railings there's a footpath that heads out across the creek-lined marsh to Canvey Point where there are excellent views right across the estuary, in particular to Leigh and Southend.

Back at the Yacht Club by the slipway that goes down to Oyster Creek, locally known as Smallgains Creek, head left

◀ A mural on the sea wall at Canvey Island

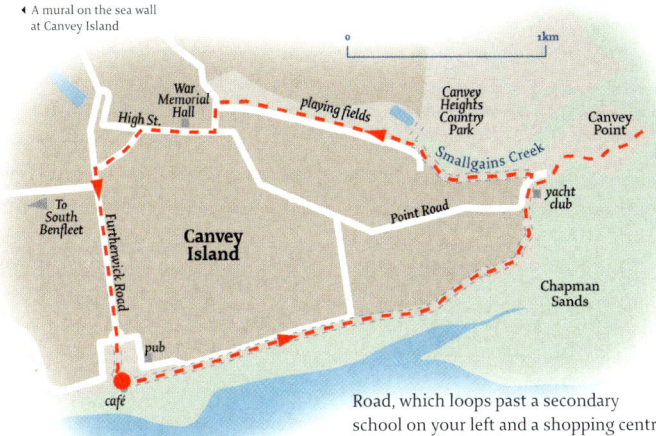

*[Map of Canvey Island showing route from café/pub near Furtherwick Road, up past High Street, War Memorial Hall, playing fields, Canvey Heights Country Park, Smallgains Creek, yacht club, Canvey Point, Chapman Sands, and back via Point Road. Scale: 0 to 1km.]*

with the sea wall on your right. Past the marina, with its very cute teashop, continue on this stone track as it bears round to the right past houseboats, yachts and dinghies to get to where it joins up with the England Coast Path. Instead of heading off down that path, you need to go left towards Smallgains Playing Field. Keep on the banked path, taking care when it dips down at various crossways until it takes a sharp right angle towards the pavilion. Step down onto the field in front and head for the corner of Mitchells Avenue where you turn left and cross over.

At the bottom of the road, turn right onto the High Street. Go past the War Memorial Hall with its Wall of Dedication and take in the hints of the East End that permeate this part of Essex. At the triple zebra crossing, head left down Foksville Road, which loops past a secondary school on your left and a shopping centre on your right.

At the end, turn left again down to Haystack Corner, named after the local pub next to the mini-roundabout, and then carry on down Furtherwick Road, past the old Rio Cinema which later became a bingo hall, to the roundabout at the bottom, where you cross over to the small gardens. Check out the huge bumblebee sculpture in the middle which pays homage to the shrill carder bee, almost extinct in other parts of the country but still quite common on the island, in particular at Canvey Wick Nature Reserve, the site of an old oil refinery on the west of the island.

Through the gardens, go past the Fun Park, across from which is the Monico pub, another example of the art deco development that first took place in the 1930s, and you're back at the Labworth where the walk started.

# Hadleigh

**Distance** 9km **Time** 2 hours 45
**Terrain** country tracks, footpaths, town
pavements **Map** OS Explorer 175
**Access** trains to Leigh-on-Sea from
Southend and London Fenchurch Street;
buses to Leigh-on-Sea from Southend

In Hadleigh, ancient and modern history merge beautifully as you step from a 13th-century castle to the site of one of the events that formed part of the 2012 Olympics. Today, Hadleigh Country Park is brimming with mountain bikers from all over the country, but there's enough space for walkers too and, with stunning views over the Thames Estuary, it would be a shame to allow the two-wheelers to have all the fun.

Start from the front of Leigh-on-Sea Station and go left up Belton Way West, past the car park, until about halfway up the hill you'll see Castle Drive going off to the left. Follow this as it narrows between bramble bushes until it reaches a gate before a field. Go through this and keep to the path on the field's right, continuing as it loops around to the right and then back round to the left. At the next corner, go over a stile towards Hadleigh Castle.

Climbing the hill offers up a rather special reward as the ruins of the castle appear in front of you above the trees. As you reach the trees, you'll see a kissing gate on your left. Go through this and then head up the hill for a closer look at the ruins. The best way to enjoy this very atmospheric place is by the rear fortifications, by the old kitchens and the Postern Gate, looking back at the main tower that remains. In front, to the left, is the Two Tree Island Nature Reserve, with the more built-up urban landscape of Canvey Island further out past the creeks and marshes.

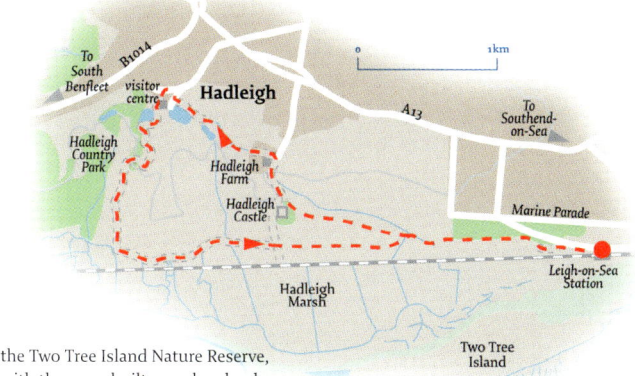

Once you've finished soaking up the views, head up to Castle Lane, an unmade track that leads up to a rare breeds centre. Up the hill, turn left and at the gates of the centre, turn right down Seaview Terrace. At the end by a small outbuilding, carry on along the path that leads to Hadleigh Country Park Visitor Centre. At various points, there are paths that lead into the country park itself but continue on this route until you reach Chapel Lane, where you turn right before turning left towards the visitor centre.

Go through the car park and past the visitor centre and at the far end of the building take the path on the right. This soon curves to the right around the mountain biking skills area before looping left around to a junction, where you turn right. It's important to try not to deviate from this path as there are plenty of tracks going off in all directions, some with very fast mountain bikers on them. In 2012, the world's elite raced across this tract of Essex with France's Julie Bresset crowned Women's Olympic Champion and Czechia's Jaroslav Kulhavy winning gold in the men's competition.

Keeping the views in front and flora mainly on your right, the path soon leads into a series of switchbacks down past the actual Olympic Racing Track, before heading over a cattle grid and then into the trees where it bears back round to the left to head southwards again.

In a while, you'll come out at a larger track where you turn left. At the next junction, turn left again to head east, ignoring any branches returning to the country park on the left. Eventually, you join a path that continues eastwards past fields and the railway line towards the bottom of the castle's high perch and back onto your original path, up Castle Drive and down to the station.

◀ The ruins of Hadleigh Castle

# Leigh to Southend

**Distance** 5.5km **Time** 1 hour 30
**Terrain** sea wall, promenades, town pavements **Map** OS Explorer 175
**Access** trains to Leigh from Southend and London Fenchurch Street; buses to Leigh from Southend; this is a linear walk, returning to the start by train

There's an element of the English Riviera about Southend as you approach from the fishing port of Leigh with palm trees, tiered gardens and art deco cafés. On a fine day, it's hard to comprehend you're not really 'on Sea' at all but at the far reaches of the Thames Estuary before it opens into the North Sea. As well as all you might expect from a popular seaside resort, Southend also lays claim to the world's longest pleasure pier.

Facing Leigh-on-Sea Station, walk down the left side and go down steps to join the High Street which runs between the railway line and Leigh Marina and then further along a row of 'sheds' selling what Leigh has always been most famous for – seafood. Beyond the concrete bridge, stick close to the seafront and you'll come across another of Leigh's popular highlights – the views across the estuary marshes and creeks.

After passing the seafront dining areas for a couple of pubs, the public right of way kicks to the left onto Alley Dock, a timeless little back lane that curves back to the High Street: turn right onto this, now in the heart of Old Leigh with its cobbled streets, weather-boarded fishermen's cottages and old taverns.

Past the sailing club, the path returns to the seafront by Bell Wharf Beach and carries on between the railway line and the sea. Some 200m on, you pass the

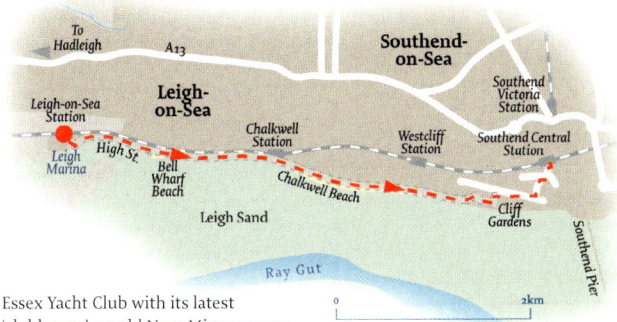

Essex Yacht Club with its latest 'clubhouse', an old Navy Minesweeper.

Go past the Cliff Bridge and then either nip onto the foreshore and under the wooden jetty or stay on the path until you reach Chalkwell Beach. This is where proper Southend starts with a lively promenade and some jaw-droppingly sumptuous beachfront homes. Taking its name from the chalkpits dug by farmers to reduce acid in the soil, it was first developed as a residential area in the early 1900s. Today, it's a delightful introduction to Southend with bowls clubs, cafés overlooking the water and an elegant esplanade perfect for walking and running, if you are so inclined.

Seamlessly morphing into the Western Esplanade, Southend town centre is not far away, although the city's 2km-long pleasure pier would have been visible for a while. Stretching into the Thames, it was originally built in 1829 after a visit from Caroline of Brunswick, the estranged wife of George IV. An iron pier replaced the timber one in 1889 with the pier railway, the first of its kind in the country, following soon after.

Now in Westcliff, and just past a kiosk where the esplanade briefly extends out towards the sea, the road to your left splits with parking spaces in between. Around 100m on, just past the archway entrance to the stairs for the Cliffs Pavilion theatre, there's a path that leads up into Southend's Cliff Gardens. Continue along the gardens, aiming for the Southend Cenotaph where you need to head up to the road above.

Turn right and carry on towards Prittlewell Gardens, which you turn into and follow around to the northeast corner. Head onto Cashiobury Terrace, past the pristine bowling green, right into Cambridge Road and then almost immediately left onto Nelson Street. At the end, turn right and after 50m, you arrive at Southend Station, where you can take a train back to the start.

◀ Southend's Cliff Gardens

Statue of Byrhtnoth in Maldon ▶

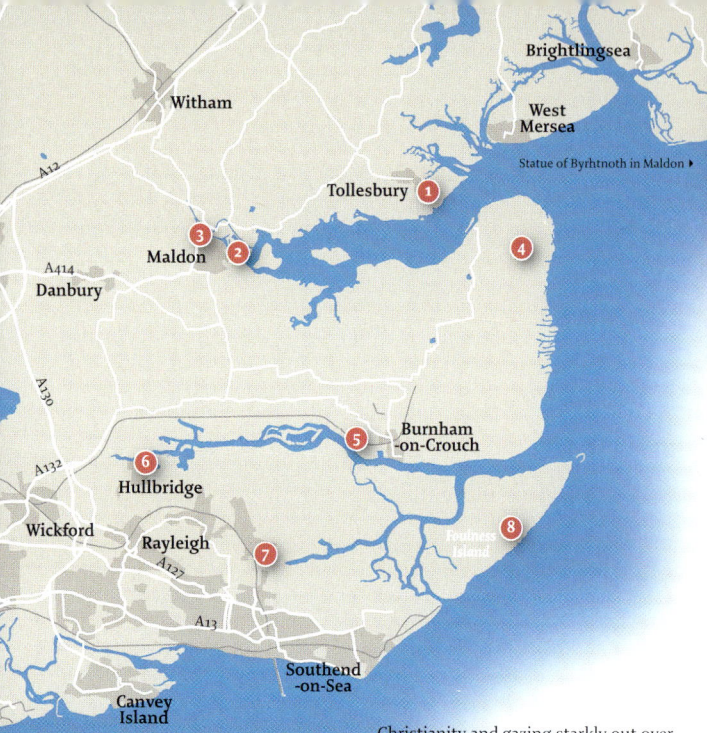

**Sparse and very much open** to the elements – in particular, the blustery North Sea – this is the county's least populated area but in places its most visually striking.

Out as far as the land will take you on the Dengie Peninsula, you'll find one of the most atmospheric churches in the country, the Chapel of St Peter-on-the-Wall, dating back to the earliest days of Christianity and gazing starkly out over the marshes towards the sea. Walking along this stretch of the Essex coast, you can be on your own for hours before seeing another rambler.

A little further north, there's a more modern-day but equally impressive edifice in the geometric form of the decommissioned Bradwell Power Station.

At either side of this area, the more populated towns of Maldon and Burnham are steeped in maritime history, with Burnham still one of the most important regattas in Britain.

# Southeast Essex

**1 Tollesbury** — 62
Take in sweeping views of saltmarsh and mudflats on this loop from a charming village

**2 Heybridge Basin** — 64
Located at the end of a navigation canal, this is a haven for pleasure boats of all shapes and sizes

**3 Maldon** — 66
Explore a lovely estuary town, full of history and surrounded by saltmarshes and waterways

**4 Bradwell-on-Sea** — 68
Stroll out on the sea wall path to reach a perfectly-sited Saxon chapel, one of the oldest in England

**5 Burnham** — 70
If you like yachts, architecture and stunning estuary views, you'll love this linear riverfront hike

**6 Hullbridge** — 72
Follow peaceful old country lanes and cross fields before returning along the estuary on this easy loop

**7 Rochford** — 74
Head out along a lesser-known estuary that's the feeding ground for an impressive range of birdlife

**8 The Broomway** — 76
Get a guide if you want to experience walking the most dangerous foreshore path in the country

# Tollesbury

**Distance** 9km **Time** 2 hours 45
**Terrain** sea wall, footpaths, pavements, country lanes **Map** OS Explorer 176
**Access** buses to Tollesbury from Colchester, Witham and Maldon

The classic image of a saltmarsh from above, with sponge-like fronds stretching out like the world's most difficult maze, is essentially the one taken over the marshes at Tollesbury. This walk is centred on the Tollesbury Wick Nature Reserve, a Site of Special Scientific Interest and a haven for wildlife. The village itself is a treat with its church square, bustling marina and a quayside with open-air saltwater lido and weather-boarded sail lofts.

Start from the centre of the village, either on the square or down East Street, and then walk up to Church Street.

Go past the church on the left and head along the country lane, past the recreation ground, until you see a metal and wooden gate and a footpath sign on the left. This path runs along a number of fields, including a very pretty tree-lined one that eventually comes out onto Mell Road, where you turn right and head down to the end of the road.

As you get to the gate, you'll see a footpath leading off to the left through some woods; go through the gate and walk along this path which widens out into a farm track that leads down to the Wick and the Tollesbury Marshes. On the way, you pass an unusual building, an old radar tower which is now a holiday let, over to your left.

Look out for a signpost and a narrow path to your right, which brings you out onto the sea wall. Turn left and then head around to the right into the Tollesbury Wick Nature Reserve, where dogs must be kept on a lead.

As you walk around the reserve, make

◁ The Sail Lofts at Tollesbury

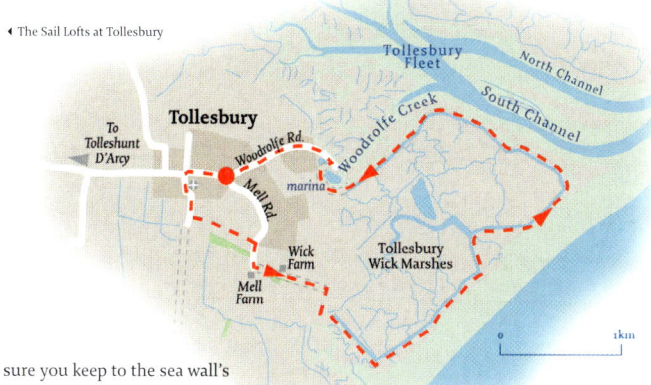

sure you keep to the sea wall's raised path as there is plenty of wildlife, including nesting birds, in the reedbeds and channel below, as well as the shoreline along the estuary.

In addition to the wildlife, there are lots of other things to look out for across the estuary, including Osea Island, which at various points has been a retreat for such artists as Stormzy and Rihanna and, of course, the stark almost Soviet-esque block buildings of Bradwell Power Station. As you walk past Blockhouse Bay and then Shinglehead Point, the sea wall path meanders back towards the village itself. Here, you can see in the distance across Tollesbury Fleet and Great Cob Island to Mersea Island.

As the path turns in again along Woodrolfe Creek, a network of rickety, narrow boardwalks suddenly appear, wandering across the marshes to the moorings of small yachts, old gaffers and dinghies. Closer to the marina, the boats get bigger and swankier, lined up alongside pristine pontoons.

The centrepiece of it all is the majestic red Trinity Lightvessel that now provides adventure activities for both young and old alike, although the 19th-century Grade II listed Granary on the slipway is a pretty striking sight itself.

Go through the gate, cross the car park and walk down the drive to find a path ahead which leads past the open-air saltwater lido. Head down the bank and then out onto Woodrolfe Road where the pale sail lofts stand with their ladders teetering on the edge of the road.

At the road, head left back up past yards and warehouses until you reach the junction to East Street and the start of your walk.

# Heybridge Basin

**Distance** 5km **Time** 1 hour 30
**Terrain** sea wall, footpaths, canal towpath
**Map** OS Explorer 183
**Access** buses to Heybridge from Colchester and Chelmsford

Heybridge Basin is where the Chelmer and Blackwater Navigation Canal meets the Blackwater Estuary. It was built in 1796 as part of the canal that ran for 22km to the Springfield Basin, by Chelmsford. This walk starts and ends on the Navigation but also takes in the estuary overlooking Northey Island where the Battle of Maldon, the subject of an Old English Poem, took place in 991AD.

Start from the Daisy Meadow car park and head up the steps to the Chelmer and Blackwater Navigation's towpath. Turn left and walk up the path towards the basin and the two locks that lead into the canal from the estuary. You'll see plenty of boats moored up here, including possibly the wondrous spectacle of a fully rigged Thames barge or two, a regular sight along the Essex estuaries in decades gone by.

Go over the canal via one of the lock gates and walk on up to the sea wall, which will take you around the flooded gravel pits, now teeming with wildfowl, gulls and waders.

Across the estuary as you walk along the wall, you'll see Northey Island, one of two large islands (the other being Osea) that dominate the landscape. This is where the Saxon Earl Byrhtnoth and his men sacrificed the high ground on Maldon Hill to fight the Vikings fairly on a 'level field', his bravery inspiring the old poem *The Battle of Maldon*.

As you head around the sea wall, you'll

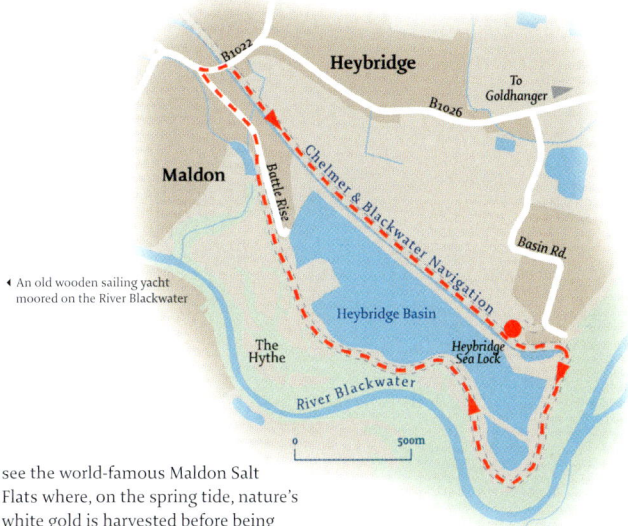

◀ An old wooden sailing yacht moored on the River Blackwater

see the world-famous Maldon Salt Flats where, on the spring tide, nature's white gold is harvested before being packed up and sent off to supermarkets and some of the country's top restaurants. On the other side of the wall is the large expanse of water that was once a gravel pit but is now a haven for cacophonous birdlife, including little egrets, herons and oystercatchers.

With marvellous views of Maldon in the distance, carry on along the sea wall path as it meanders its way back to civilisation, past some new-builds on your right and industrial units on your left.

The path is still raised but narrows here as it slips through blackthorn hedging until you come out on the driveway of a house, which leads onto Hall Road. It soon becomes quite industrial with warehouses, yards and factories, including the old site of Bentalls Agricultural Ironworks where the first steam-powered threshing machine was built. When you reach the main B1022 road, turn right, go over the bridge and then head back down onto the Chelmer and Blackwater Navigation on your right.

If you were to walk back under the bridge here and follow the canal's towpath around to the Blackwater Rail Trail and the Mill Lane Footbridge, you would be able to link up with the Maldon walk (overleaf) for an extended day out.

To complete this walk, however, carry on along the Navigation, taking in the moored barges, cruisers and houseboats as you make your way back to the basin and the car park.

# Maldon

**Distance** 8.5km **Time** 2 hours 30
**Terrain** town pavements, footpaths,
canal towpaths **Map** OS Explorer 183
**Access** buses to Maldon from Colchester
and Chelmsford

This pretty estuary town has a thriving centre, as well as some of the best surrounding countryside the county has to offer with its saltmarshes, network of waterways and rambling fields and woodland. Promenade Park has a cornucopia of attractions for both young and old, while the historic Hythe Quay takes you back to when Maldon was a bustling port.

The walk starts in the expansive Promenade Park, heading from the car park to the far end of the promenade where you can walk out to the spur and pay a visit to Byrhtnoth, the hero of the Battle of Maldon in 991AD.

Return along the promenade into Hythe Quay with its Thames sailing barges and walk up the hill, crossing to Downs Road, which passes a small green before winding round to the left. At the corner, leave it to go straight ahead and down to Chandlers Quay, keeping to the path and then, when you reach the houses on the quay, keeping the front doors on your right. This leads you to Anchorage Hill and then Fullbridge, where you turn left and go up Market Hill.

Halfway up the hill, cross over and turn right, continuing up Cromwell Hill. At the top, turn right down Beeleigh Road. Near the end of the road, keep an eye out for the start of a fenced public footpath that runs parallel to the road. Take this to emerge at the bottom of Dykes Chase where you carry straight on past the house of Hillyfield and the field on your left, continuing down the path where you'll hear the traffic from the Maldon bypass. You can cross this dual-carriageway but it's better to take the footpath loop that goes under the road and then back up. At this point, go right, through the woods and down to Beeleigh Abbey. This used to be the site of a monastery but is now a private residence once owned by William Foyle, co-founder of Foyles Bookshop in London; he formed one of the most substantial English private libraries of the 20th century here.

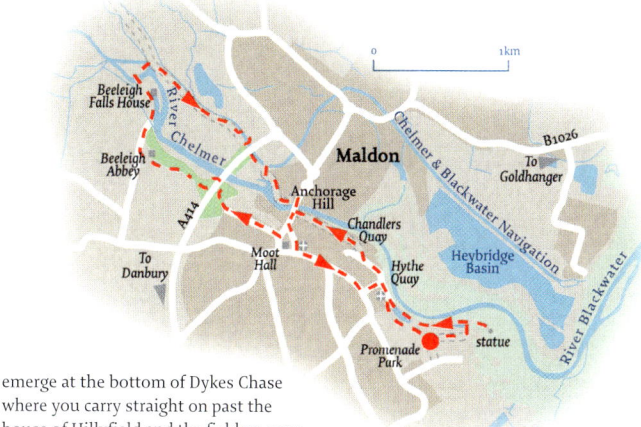

After the gravel parking area, turn right down the country lane and carry straight on past the No Entry sign to Beeleigh Falls House, a splendid Victorian building with an ornate metal veranda frontage. Carry on past the property through the gate which gives access to the 'falls' themselves, a collection of roaring weirs.

Once over the bridge, keep the river on your right as you make your way up to the canal, turning right here and going over the weir to head past the golf club. Back under the main carriageway, you'll soon see a footbridge and a path to your right. Take this and climb up onto the cycleway and footpath, before turning left and walking back towards Maldon.

Go past the pub and then right through the parking area of Bridge Court and the back of Bridge Cottages, before going over the zebra crossing and heading back up Market Hill, this time to the top. To your left is Thomas Plume's Library which consists of 8000 books and pamphlets, belonging to the Greenwich vicar who bequeathed the collection to his home town on his death in 1704. If you go right down the High Street you'll find the wonderful old Moot Hall. You need to turn left, though, and carry on down the High Street until you reach North Street, which takes you back down to Hythe Quay and then on to Promenade Park.

◀ Down the River Chelmer Estuary to Maldon

# Bradwell-on-Sea

**Distance** 10km **Time** 3 hours 15 **Terrain** town pavements, footpaths, sea wall **Map** OS Explorer 176 **Access** buses to Bradwell-on-Sea from Maldon and Burnham-on-Crouch

There's plenty to enjoy on this walk, such as the picturesque village of Bradwell with its timber-framed pub, Arts and Crafts hall and its church dating back to the 14th century. That would be a pretty impressive ecclesiastical draw in itself if it wasn't for the chapel at the end of a stone track beyond the village, one of the oldest, most important and arguably most atmospheric in the country.

Start from Bradwell-on-Sea which, despite its name, is actually a good 3km away from the sea. From the church on the High Street, walk down East End Road, past the tree-lined graveyard with its pretty lychgate. Carry on walking along the pavement, through a more modern residential development, until you emerge in an open area with a field on your right. Opposite a black weather-boarded house is Hockley Lane, where you turn right.

Carry on down this country lane, past a cul-de-sac of homes on your right and then a collection of agricultural barns and outbuildings. The lane then winds its serpentine way down to the marsh and sea wall, through a metal gate and past a windfarm of statuesque turbines. At a sharp right, there's what remains of a farmhouse and at the end of the lane another smallholding with a farmhouse and more outbuildings.

As you reach the corner protected by a clump of trees, turn left towards the sea; this is where you join St Peter's Way, a 72km long-distance path that makes its way from Chipping Ongar, predominantly through countryside, avoiding many of the county's larger built-up areas.

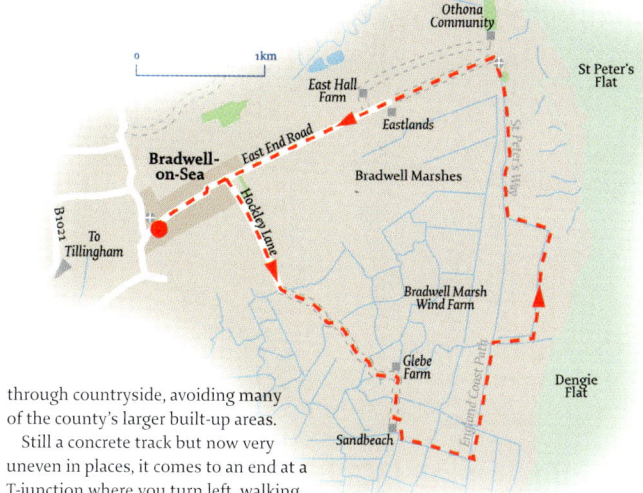

Still a concrete track but now very uneven in places, it comes to an end at a T-junction where you turn left, walking alongside a field until you come to the raised sea wall, which separates the saltmarsh and the sea from the arable fields behind it. At various points in the year, the entire sea wall path, which runs from Bradwell Waterside all the way round the Dengie Peninsula to Burnham, can either be overgrown (summer) or muddy and uneven (winter) so do take care. That said, it's worth the struggle either way for the spectacular views across the marshes and out over the sandflats.

Carry on along the sea wall, or the grass path that runs below it, until you reach a copse of trees, behind which lies the simple but breathtakingly austere Chapel of St Peter-on-the-Wall. It was built by Bishop Cedd in 654AD out of the ruins of the Roman fort of Othona and quickly became an important religious centre. Although it was disused for many hundreds of years, at one point being used as a barn, it now holds regular weekly services, as well as concerts and other events. Behind the church is the Othona Christian Community, which was founded in 1946 and still hosts courses and retreats today.

From the chapel, head west on the stone track that leads to a large car park and the road beyond. This road has no path to speak of, so take care walking along it until you reach Hockley Lane, where you can pick up the pavement that leads back into the village and the start.

◀ The Chapel of St Peter-on-the-Wall

# Burnham

**Distance** 9km **Time** 2 hours 45
**Terrain** sea wall, town pavements and riverside paths **Map** OS Explorer 176
**Access** trains to Burnham from Shenfield and Southend; buses to Burnham from Chelmsford; this is a linear walk, returning by train

After Cowes on the Isle of Wight, the most prestigious of England's yachting weeks is Burnham, and just walking along the riverfront you can see why. Along with the chalet-style Burnham Sailing Club and the glass-fronted Royal Burnham Yacht Club, there's the famous clubhouse of the Royal Corinthian Yacht Club, a rare example in Britain of the International Style of architecture.

Start the walk at Althorne Station after getting a train there from Burnham. Leaving the station, turn right and cross the level crossing, continuing down this unmade road which takes you to the riverfront and the first of many marinas you'll see on this walk. Just before the entrance, you'll see the sea wall hugging the fence running off to your left. Step up and take the sea wall path east towards the riverfront itself, across which is Bridgemarsh Island. This stretch of water is Althorne Creek which, after the path has made a lovely loop around a lagoon, soon drifts into the wide estuary of the River Crouch.

Inland there's a more recent addition to the Essex countryside – acres of vineyards, growing a variety of Pinot Noir, Pinot Gris and Chardonnay grapes. A little further along the sea wall, the path temporarily diverts inland, heading up and along a field. Locally known as the Cliff, it offers spectacular views of the estuary upstream to Fambridge and the other way towards Wallasea Island, with Burnham as yet hidden around the bend of the river.

Carry on down the hill and back along

◀ The Royal Corinthian Yacht Club at Burnham-on-Crouch

the narrow path on the sea wall which brings you into Creeksea with its very enviable properties; the location of one of these means you have to head inland once again. At the back gate of this property, turn left down through a clump of trees and through a wooden gate into a field. Turn right and continue alongside the field until you reach another gate which leads into Ferry Road. Head right and back down to the river by the Creaksea Sailing Club, where you continue to the end of the road and along the shore past the front of some more spectacular riverside homes.

This section gives you your first view of Burnham and, in particular, the distant Corinthian Clubhouse. Built in 1931, this was the country's contribution to the International Exhibition of Modern Architecture held the following year in New York.

Head around the Burnham yacht harbour, with more symbols of wealth and luxury, this time in the form of cruisers and yachts, looping back on yourself on the other side, where the path is wider and more like a promenade.

After passing grand houseboats, keep to the path as it winds round jetties, moorings and boathouses until it comes into the Quay and a row of smart 18th-century brick and timber houses and pubs with white-silled bays and dormers looking out at the river.

Carry on along the pretty waterfront until the path comes out onto a driveway off Belvedere Road, where you'll see the Corinthian up close.

Head left onto the road and continue up to the High Street where you turn left again. This runs parallel to the waterfront but offers up equally wonderful sights, such as the town's octagonal Victorian clocktower which you can walk through.

Carry on along the High Street as it bears right and up into Station Road for around 1km until you see the entrance to the station on your left.

# Hullbridge

**Distance** 4km **Time** 1 hour
**Terrain** town pavements, sea wall, country lanes and footpaths
**Map** OS Explorer 175 **Access** buses to Hullbridge from Southend

Tucked away along the narrowing estuary of the River Crouch, Hullbridge is so called because of the old name for the river and the bridge that once crossed it. Much like many other settlements in this part of the county, Hullbridge has a Plotlands feel to it with the gridlike roads of the holiday and residential parks. But out on the river and along old country lanes, the real magic of the place can be discovered.

Start from the large car park which is situated on Ferry Road and then go left down Pooles Lane, which leads past the entrances to several residential and holiday parks before getting to the village's recreation ground on the left. Just before that, on the right, is a signpost pointing to a path that follows a hedgerow down past a field. As you continue, this path has an almost manicured feel as though it is leading you through a country house maze.

Eventually, it comes out onto a residential street, where you turn right and then left down Burnham Road. After Pinewood Close, follow the next footpath signpost between garden fences to a wooden bridge over a ditch and into a field. The path skirts alongside it, bringing you out onto a gravel track, where you head left.

After passing Cracknell's Farm and another house and farm outbuildings further up, the track narrows and becomes more enclosed with trees bending overhead. This atmospheric byway is part of the Saffron Trail, a 112km

◀ River Crouch at Hullbridge

route that links up Southend in the southeast with Saffron Walden in the northwest.

The path comes out onto a country road, where you carry straight on before it hooks round to the left. Just up on your right, there's a metal gate which leads into the recreation ground. Keep to the right-hand side and make your way up to the sea wall that overlooks the Crouch.

From here, you can head off right as an extension to this walk along a line of very swanky riverfront homes, some with their own private jetties, and carry on to Brandy Hole. Past the moorings, there's a wonderful stretch of footpath that sneaks in and out of dense blackthorn, very narrow and very uneven, with occasional glimpses of the creek-lined saltmarsh outside. It's a little like a location you might find in a *Pirates of the Caribbean* movie – mysterious, dark but exciting nonetheless.

Unfortunately, despite showing such promise (and there being a clear route indicated on the OS map as heading inland along the creek), this path doesn't ultimately lead anywhere, because as it comes out into the open and meanders towards the Reach, it abruptly ends, thanks to river erosion and the myriad channels that snake inland from the Crouch. Of course, this makes the detour even more secluded and peaceful.

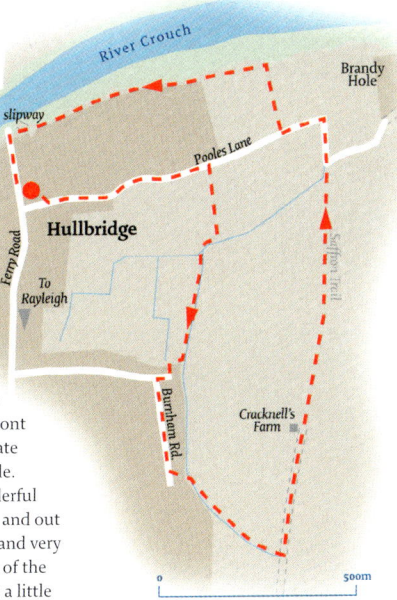

If you do make the detour, retrace your steps to the recreation ground and the sea wall and then continue along the shore towards the centre of Hullbridge itself. Pass more holiday homes, go through some narrow hedgerows, and then further along at the second of two slipways turn left up the hill on Ferry Road and you will find the car park on your left at the start.

# Rochford

**Distance** 11km **Time** 3 hours 45
**Terrain** town pavements, sea wall, fields, country lanes **Map** OS Explorer 175
**Access** buses to Rochford from Southend; trains to Rochford from Shenfield and Southend

This route explores a microcosm of the county itself – part industrial urban landscape, part picturesque wilderness. At times it's swarming with traffic and people with the far-off clanking of cranes echoing all round, and at others it's just you, the smell of salt brine and a lone oystercatcher trilling overhead. The Roach is perhaps the least well known of the estuaries in these parts, which is why it's perfect escapist country.

Start from Rochford Station car park and turn right, going over the pedestrian crossing and continuing up West Street at the mini-roundabout to soon pass the town's Market Square. At the end of the road, cross over and then walk left up East Street until you reach Rocheway on your right. Take this residential street to the end, where you carry on along a path that goes through a field. At the end, turn right down Mill Lane and almost immediately head left along another path which forms part of the Roach Valley Way. Walk between some densely wooded fishing ponds before intersecting a cricket ground. Across the narrow driveway, go right down a footpath that leads to the River Roach itself and then turn left along the sea wall.

Within minutes, you feel like you're in the middle of nowhere, with only a few houses and farm buildings scattered beyond the sea wall path.

Carry on along the estuary beside its rich fields of saltmarsh plantlife, including the favourite of many a London

◂ The River Roach just outside Rochford

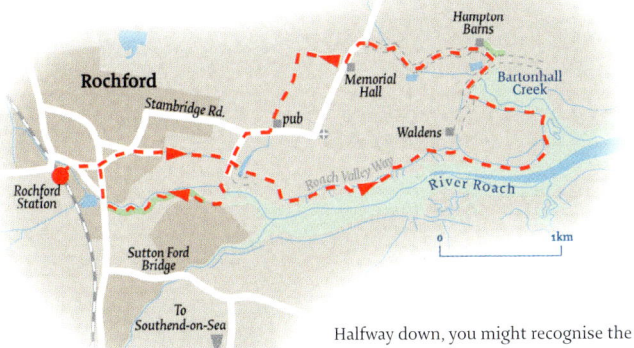

chef – samphire. The path follows a zigzag route along the river as it gently widens, before slipping inland and around Bartonhall Creek, an inlet that would have been spectacularly perfect for smugglers.

At the far end, follow the gravel track below and when it reaches Hampton Barns Lane, step down from the path and head left down the road.

This goes past a little collection of houses before fields and then industrial units at the end. At the main road, take great care crossing and then go left along the pavement. Around the corner and opposite the Memorial Hall, take the footpath that leads alongside a field to the hedgerow, where you take a left turn down to the Cherry Tree pub. Go right along the main road and then down Mill Lane on your left, again taking care as you cross the road.

Halfway down, you might recognise the lane as the one you crossed earlier in the walk, but this time carry straight on to the path near the bottom and on your right. This path also forms part of the Roach Valley Way and curves round past the derelict remains of Stambridge Mill with its huge silos covered in colourful graffiti.

Cross the bridge directly south of the mill site to a densely wooded path that heads right, following the river as it narrows to a creek. This is a fine secretive part of the walk, with the brief glimpses of shipping containers and shelves of cars your only clue to the existence of a huge industrial estate on your left.

Eventually, the path leads out to a track and then the town of Rochford itself. Head right and then right again up South Street, which takes you back to West Street on your left. Turn down this, past the market, to find the Southend main road and the station car park where the walk started.

# The Broomway

A volume of Essex Walks just wouldn't be complete without an entry for what is perhaps the county's most famous walk – or rather, infamous. In recent years, The Broomway has been gathering more headlines for the fact it is Britain's most dangerous footpath with more than 100 people losing their lives on it. While there are no precise accounts of the exact number of deaths in its long history, there are plenty of reasons to take this figure seriously.

Firstly, it's a footpath that runs out into the sea – at low tide, of course – along the Maplin Sands, connecting the mainland at Wakering Stairs to Foulness Island. Up until 1922, when a bridge was built at Havengore Creek, it was the only access to the island by foot or horse and cart, so it was well used on a daily basis. As you might expect from a footpath that runs along the sands, the main danger is from the fast-flowing incoming tide, which because of the mouths of the Rivers Crouch and Roach can cause whirlpools in places.

Then there's the ever changing pockets of quicksand to avoid sinking into, not to mention any unexploded ordnance from the artillery testing ranges run by the Ministry of Defence nearby.

This is all part of the attraction – the secrecy, the danger, but also the sheer magic of stepping out onto a mirror where the reflections of the sky merge with the water on the horizon.

The Broomway runs for almost 10km and is so named because of the 'brooms' – or bundles of twigs attached to short poles – which were planted into the mud to mark out the way. Unfortunately, the brooms are no longer there so, in terms of waymarkers, there is very little to help the modern-day traveller where to go or, more importantly, where not to go. The only real point out on the sands is the Maypole, which is little more than a huge post with wooden planks nailed up and down its length.

Because of the perilous nature of walking it, and because access to Foulness and Wakering Stairs itself is often restricted because of firing tests, it is strongly recommended that anyone who wants to walk The Broomway must take a guide, easily found online by searching for 'Broomway Guide'.

As well as keeping you safe, they have plenty of local information, which you would expect from any good guide. That said, some of the best moments are when you hold back a little, letting the rest of the group wander on and giving you time to revel in the tranquillity of the sights and sounds of literally walking on water.

Walkers heading towards the Havengore Maypole

**In this corner of the county,** a walker can pretty much enjoy all Essex has to offer – from ancient history to striking natural vistas and a cultural hotspot or two. Here, you will find the birthplace of the *Mayflower*, the ship that took the Pilgrim Fathers to America, as well as the nursery rhyme capital of the world, the oldest and longest Roman town wall in England and a spectacular work of art/architecture by a Turner Prize-winning artist.

World-famous oysterbeds, world-famous saltflats, world-famous jams, there's also plenty of culinary sustenance to fuel adventures along creeks, through fields and across streams and brooks.

As West Essex provides the perfect introduction to the county, so discovering the highways and byways of Northeast Essex is the ideal way to round up your exploration. From voices from the ancient past lurking on city street corners to breathtaking images of fragile estuarine landscapes, there are always more surprises to uncover along the way.

# Northeast Essex

**1 Coggeshall** — 80
Take in some fantastic Tudor architecture before circling around the surrounding countryside

**2 Fordham Heath to West Bergholt** — 82
Stroll alongside the meandering River Colne and through the largest new woodland in the east of England

**3 Colchester** — 84
Unsurprisingly for the first major city in Roman Britain, there's plenty of historical interest on this quick tour

**4 West Mersea** — 86
Loop around the west coast before sampling the locally-grown oysters and returning along a lovely beach

**5 Wivenhoe** — 88
Experience the saltmarsh, expansive estuary views and mixed woodland on this easy circuit

**6 Mistley to Wrabness** — 90
Witchfinding and househunting both feature on this linear walk along the south bank of the Stour Estuary

**7 Walton-on-the-Naze** — 92
Head out from a charming seaside town to investigate wild heathland, saltmarshes and sandy beaches

**8 Harwich to Dovercourt** — 94
Fascinating history combines with sublime seascapes on this stroll through Essex's most northerly coastal town

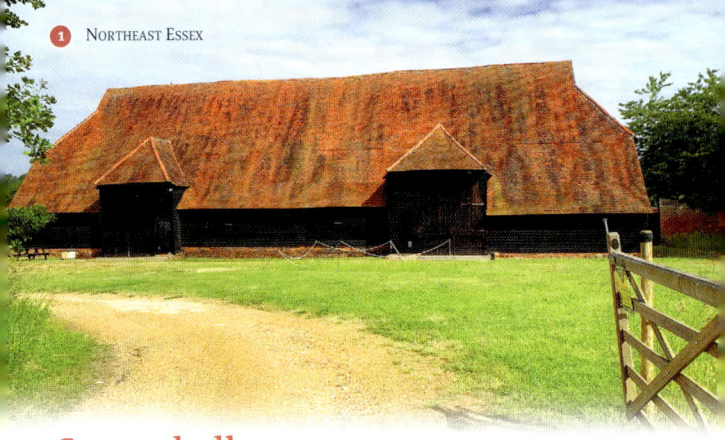

# Coggeshall

**Distance** 6km **Time** 2 hours
**Terrain** pavements, country tracks, fields **Map** OS Explorer 195
**Access** buses to Coggeshall from Colchester and Braintree

When it comes to history, Coggeshall punches way above its weight, with almost 300 listed buildings within its small town centre. These include the National Trust's Paycocke's House, built around 1500 by a wealthy cloth merchant, and 13th-century Grange Barn, one of the oldest timber-framed buildings in Europe. As well as passing these architectural gems, this walk follows some of the Essex Way, the county's longest continuous path.

Start from the town's main car park in Stoneham Street and head through the alley onto Market Hill where, across the road to the left, restaurateur Peter Langan of Langan's Brasserie fame set up an eaterie in the 1980s, bringing Parisian café society to Coggeshall. Now called Ranfield's Brasserie, it is still a high-end restaurant. Turn right and head down towards the White Hart, where you cross the road and then go left down Bridge Street. As you make your way out of the town centre, look left down a narrow alley and you'll see the buildings that once made up the Victorian Coggeshall Brewery. Go over the bridge which gives the street its name, crossing the River Blackwater with sweeping willows and lush green watermeadows either side.

Carry on along the pavement on the left-hand side until you reach Coggeshall Hamlet, where you cross the main road, taking the country lane on your right. Follow this round to the left and then at the Y-junction go right. This lane meanders beside open fields with views back down to Coggeshall in the distance. Ignore any paths branching off until you reach the point where a footpath crosses the road, with a farm track on your left; head right, across a field, here. This leads into another field and then eventually to a long line of thick hedgerow – through a gap you'll find a stone track that forms part of the Essex Way. Turn right to follow this and carry on until you reach a signpost that directs you down to Nunn's Bridge. It's worth a detour down to this charming footbridge, built by local blacksmith Henry Nunn in 1892 and recently restored after being saved from demolition by local residents.

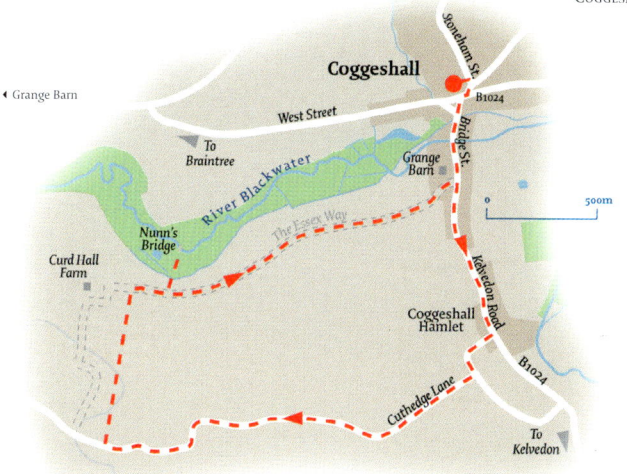

Back up on the Essex Way, carry on along the stone track heading into the town to pass Grange Farm, which is Tudor in origin but has splendid Georgian additions, not to mention an incredibly ornate French oak door.

Just round the corner is the pick of the buildings on this walk, Grange Barn, now run by the National Trust. It was built by the Cistercian order of monks and, as well as being one of the oldest of its type in Europe, it's also one of the biggest at 36m long and nearly 11m high. After the dissolution of the abbey in the 1530s, the barn was used for agricultural purposes right up until the 1960s when it fell into disrepair before being rescued first by the local council and then the National Trust.

From the entrance to Grange Barn, walk to the main road and then turn left down the hill and over the bridge. This is a pretty riverside spot with a swan memorial bench on the left if you wish to pause before you return to the town centre. From here, retrace your steps to the start.

# Fordham Heath to West Bergholt

**Distance** 10km **Time** 3 hours 15
**Terrain** country tracks, fields, footpaths
**Map** OS Explorer 184 **Access** buses to
Fordham from Colchester

This walk starts and ends at Fordham Hall Estate which, thanks to the work of the Woodland Trust, is the largest woodland creation site in the East of England with 250,000 trees planted and more than 200 hectares of Open Access Land to explore. Towards West Bergholt, a stop-off at St Mary's Old Church, now run by the Churches Conservation Trust, is a must. Climb the stairs to reach an 18th-century gallery overlooking the Chancel Arch and the striking fresco of the Arms of James I above.

Start from the Woodland Trust's car park off Ponders Road and head back onto the main road towards the T-junction with Church Road. Turn right and then cross over by the footpath sign which leads into a play area and fields. Walk to the end, where you go through a gap in the hedge to a wooded area. Take the path straight across and continue along it until it comes out opposite a house and a farm track. Cross the track to continue around the left-hand side of the house and then in a northeasterly direction up to the country lane.

Turn right and walk along the lane until you reach another T-junction, where you go right. About 300m along on your left, you'll see a footpath sign, where you walk along the edge of a field. At the end, there's the tiniest of gaps which you go through before continuing in the same direction and then carrying straight on across another field. This leads down to the corner of a hedgerow where you continue onwards, alongside another field to a gap in the hedge at the bottom.

Once through, head right and uphill, skirting the edge of Hillhouse Woods. This eventually brings you onto a stone farm track which winds round more

◀ An ancient oak on the Essex Way

woods and fields before leading to the atmospheric St Mary's Old Church.

As you head right on the lane, notice the magnificent Georgian-built West Bergholt Hall, before nipping through the trees to the track which is where you pick up the Essex Way. Head down the track to Cooks Hall Road, which leads round to a modern barn conversion. Bear right and then left, keeping the building on your left. This track continues past fields, gates and hedgerows before crossing a bridge over a stream and into a field with a grand oak tree at the end. Aim for the left-hand corner, go through a gap and continue ahead with the River Colne sweeping snake-like to your left. Across the banks, you'll see a number of pillboxes, the remnants of the Second World War Eastern Command Line.

Once you pass through a gate, you're back in the Fordham Hall Estate. Follow the path that forms the southern end of the estate until you get to Mill Road, which you need to take care crossing. Then keep on the path, ignoring the numerous metal gates of the estate on your right, before it bears round to the right, past the back of the Shoulder of Mutton licensed tearoom and houses.

Eventually, the path leads round to the right again and, at the first chance to cross the road, do so, again taking care as this section can be quite fast. Back on the estate, the path leads right and up through meadows lined with hedgerows and trees in the distance. This path gently sweeps to the right as it nears a thick line of trees and brings you back to the car park where the walk started.

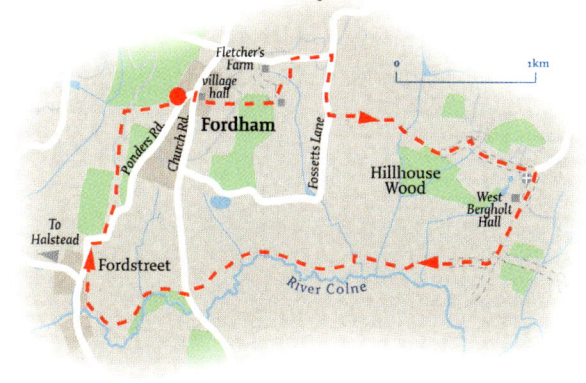

# Colchester

**Distance** 3.5km **Time** 1 hour
**Terrain** town pavements and park paths
**Map** OS Explorer 184 **Access** trains to Colchester from Ipswich, Chelmsford and London Liverpool Street

Colchester has quite an impressive list of historical firsts – including Britain's oldest recorded city, thanks to accounts by Roman authors Pliny the Elder and Tacitus, and Europe's largest Norman keep, built around 1076 on top of Britain's largest Roman temple, dedicated to the Emperor Claudius. Then there's Britain's oldest and longest Roman town wall which this walk passes, as well as one of the oldest Scouting Groups and Jumbo, the largest watertower.

Start from the Britannia car park near Colchester Town Station and head north through the gate, past St Botolph's Church on your left and then up into St Botolph's Priory, one of the first Augustinian priories in England, dating back to 1093. The steps and path take you into Priory Street, where you get your first view of the city's Roman wall in front of you and heading off to the right. Go in the opposite direction to the end of the road where you turn right and walk up to join Queen Street, continuing uphill until you reach a side road on your right. Follow the road around, where you'll see the striking gold curved roof of the city's art gallery, Firstsite, known locally as the 'Golden Banana'. Walk up Lewis Gardens next to The Minories, another art gallery, on your left. At the end, turn right and carry on down East Hill until you reach the Church of St James the Great.

Cross the road and walk along Roman Road to the top, where you'll see the wall again. Head left with the road, then go through the archway onto the path and head left alongside the wall past Duncan's Gate to reach another gap in the wall. Go through this and head up through the park, past the café on your left and the rather lovely Victorian bandstand on your right. Keep left, then carry straight on and up the hill until you see a Georgian mansion in front of a lawn. This is Hollytrees, a museum and also the city's visitor information centre.

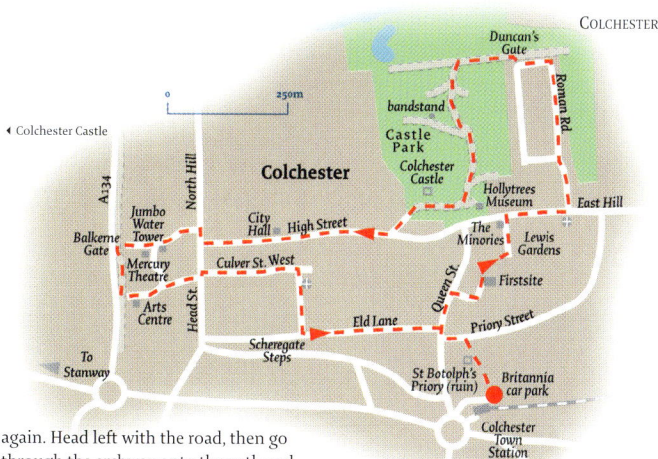

Head right and around to be greeted by the magnificent Colchester Castle, another museum containing stacks of Roman artefacts. Carry on through the park gates and go straight down Museum Street to emerge on the city's High Street, where you turn right.

Walk past the shops and bars, taking notice of two of the city's oldest buildings, the George Hotel and the Red Lion Hotel. Go past the grand City Hall and cross over at the top of North Hill. Head downhill before turning left down Balkerne Passage, which brings you round to the Victorian Jumbo Water Tower and the more recently built Mercury Theatre.

Head through the Balkerne Gate, the largest surviving Roman gateway in Britain, which dates back to the second century, and turn left, walking alongside the Roman wall until you reach a set of steps going up and through a gap. This leads past the Colchester Arts Centre and down Church Street to Head Street, where you cross over into Culver Street West.

At the end, you'll see Trinity Church, which is Saxon in origin. Go right down Trinity Street and then left at the end, past Scheregate Steps, one of the medieval gateways that used to cut through the Roman wall. Continue along Eld Lane until you reach Queen Street. Cross over here, turn right and then go left back down Priory Street, returning through the priory to arrive back at the car park at the start.

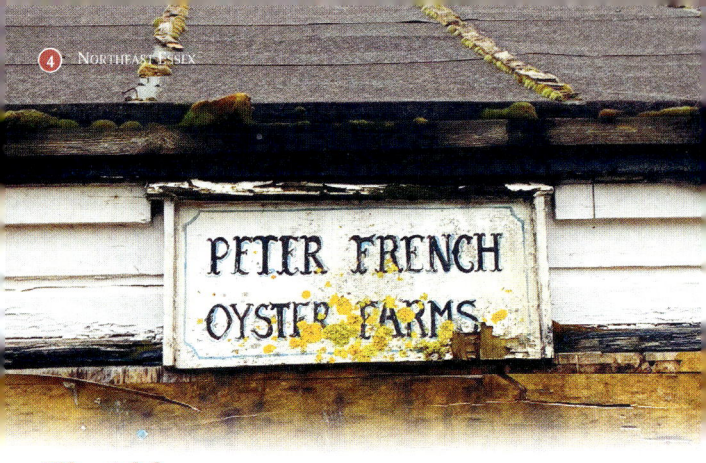

# West Mersea

Distance 6km Time 2 hours
Terrain pavements, footpaths, tracks
Map OS Explorer 184 Access buses to West Mersea from Colchester. Check tide times before leaving as the road across to the island can get flooded

Mersea Island is renowned the world over for its Colchester Native Oysters, but it also offers a whole range of seafood, freshly served up within hours of being landed, so make sure you visit one of the many shacks selling the local fruits of the sea. As well as food, it's a mecca for maritime activity, the pinging of halyards providing a pleasing metronomic soundtrack to this walk, especially on the waterfront in a prevailing breeze.

Start at the Willoughby Avenue car park, a large meadow, which can get pretty busy in the height of summer, and head north out onto Oakwood Avenue. Take care crossing East Road and continue up the avenue until you reach the end, where there's a gap to the left that leads out onto the main road into West Mersea. Turn left and keep to the pavement. Further on, at the next corner sweeping left onto Mill Road, you need to cross over to continue on Colchester Road: it is a sharp bend and it's best to cross further round the corner, then double back on the other side.

Carry on past houses on the left and views of fields sweeping down to the Strood Channel on your right until you can see another left-hand bend up ahead. This time cross the road before you reach the bend and continue on the opposite pavement past the bowling club entrance to the adjacent drive with footpath sign. Turn onto this to pass a couple of houses and join the footpath which leads along the back of a residential estate after the drive ends.

Continue on this path until there's a

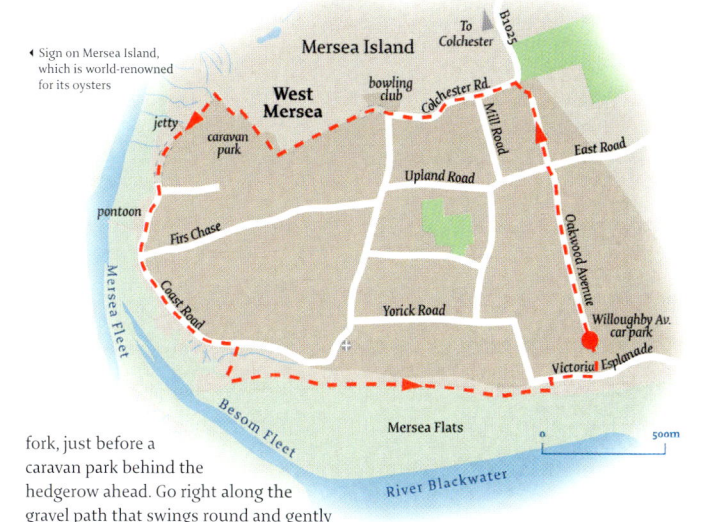

◀ Sign on Mersea Island, which is world-renowned for its oysters

fork, just before a caravan park behind the hedgerow ahead. Go right along the gravel path that swings round and gently drops to the saltmarsh and creeks below.

At the end, go left past the old wooden jetty and along the concrete sea wall until you get to one of two yacht clubs on the West Mersea front. Swing round and onto the main coast road, which leads past boatyards, oyster sheds and pretty old fishermen's cottages.

Further along, there's the dazzling frontage of the other yacht club, a couple of pubs, and more seafood shacks to enjoy Mersea's culinary contribution to the county.

As you continue along the road, the yachts are replaced by grand houseboats comfortably sunk into the cracks of the ribbons of creeks that unfurl through the saltmarsh.

Just after this, there's a footpath that leads toward the shoreline itself, over a narrow boardwalk to the beach. Taking care that you've got the tide right, head left with views across the water and some spectacular beachfront homes on your inland side.

Sand, shingle and even the odd oyster shell provide a satisfying crunch as you gently plod up to the line of cheerful beach huts that stretch down from Victoria Esplanade off in the distance.

At the first major gap in the huts, there's a set of steps that lead up to a café. Go up and around the stairs to the road, crossing this to get back to the car park.

It is possible to walk all the way around Mersea Island, depending on the tides, and even though it's a good 20km, it's definitely worth taking a whole day for it.

# Wivenhoe

**Distance** 6.5km **Time** 2 hours
**Terrain** town pavements, footpaths (some muddy), country tracks
**Map** OS Explorer 184 **Access** buses to Wivenhoe from Colchester; trains to Wivenhoe from Colchester and Clacton

You can understand why Wivenhoe, or *Wyven Hoe* (Dragon's Lair), was the location of choice for the filmmakers of Sarah Perry's award-winning novel, *The Essex Serpent*. It has all the constituent ingredients – wide open stretches of water, meandering capillary-like rivulets of saltmarsh and footpaths that slip into deep dark woodland.

The town itself has a romantic history of smuggling and shipbuilding, while in more recent years it has become a melting pot for the local and national arts scene. Francis Bacon had a studio here while Joan Hickson, best known for her role in Agatha Christie's *Miss Marple* in the 1980s television series, made her home just off the town's picturesque Quay.

Start from the town's railway station car park and make your way to the far end, where the Wivenhoe Trail begins. This beautiful trail takes walkers and cyclists back towards Colchester, but for this walk take the boarded ramp to your left up to a residential street. Turn right and head beneath a black weather-boarded house to Spindrift Way. Bordered by reedbeds scattered with tiny birds on your right and nautically decorated houses on your left, carry on towards Old Ferry Road, where you turn right. Follow this road round until you see a footpath sign on your right, which takes you down West Quay. Now a riverside housing estate, this used to be Wivenhoe's Old Port.

With sweeping views across the River Colne to Rowhedge, carry on along the front towards the town's Quay. Here, you'll find the Nottage Institute, where you can still take courses on boatbuilding and yacht skippering, while further along is another new development where the famous James W Cook Shipyard once stood. You can see what's left of the town's once vibrant fishing fleet here and at the end of the jetty, there are excellent views across to Fingringhoe and of the Colne Flood Barrier, completed in 1994.

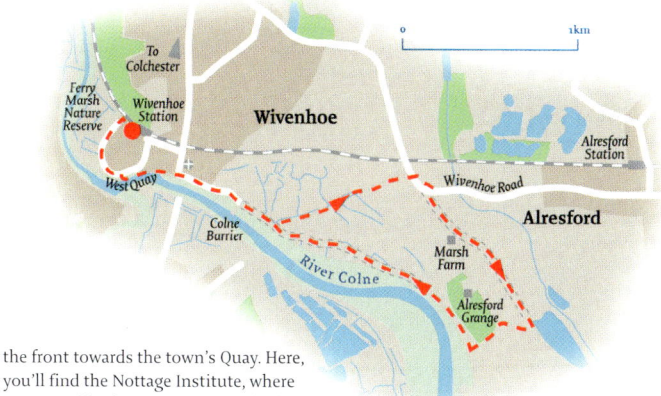

Head downriver towards the sailing club and pass through the gates. The raised riverside path stretches far off into the distance, following the estuary down to Alresford Creek but, well before that, head inland across grassy marshland to a raised bank in the distance. Don't worry about missing out on the spectacular views of the estuary – the walk comes back down the riverside path.

Up the steps and across the bank where the old Wivenhoe to Brightlingsea railway used to run before the Beeching cuts, carry straight on through towering reeds and another gate, and up a line of trees to the main road. Cross over and head right for a while, before crossing back over on the bend to an old quarry track. Keep to the right of the quarry road and walk on past Alresford Grange and its picturesque parkland gardens until you see a metal gate with a yellow-arrowed footpath marker on your right. This takes you to a field, where you need to turn right and then follow the path round in a slow looping left turn, which eventually leads you through trees and down a steep stepped hill to the wooded riverside path. Turn right again and carry on, taking care of your footing over the many tree roots on the ground, before the path emerges from the trees into the open.

This is the raised footpath that eventually leads back into the town of Wivenhoe. Either retrace your steps to the railway car park or explore the narrow streets of the pretty town before returning to the start.

◀ Along the River Colne towards Wivenhoe

# Mistley to Wrabness

**Distance** 10km **Time** 3 hours 15 **Terrain** footpaths, sea wall, fields, country lanes **Map** OS Explorer 184 **Access** buses to Mistley from Colchester, Clacton and Harwich; trains to Mistley from Colchester and London Liverpool Street; this is a linear walk, returning to the start by train

This walk passes one of the county's most extraordinary buildings – Grayson Perry's A House For Essex – with views along the way that sweep across the Stour Estuary to the Shotley Peninsula and the spectacular frontage of the 'Cradle of the Navy', the Royal Hospital School at Holbrook. The walk starts in Mistley, the former home of notorious Witchfinder General, Matthew Hopkins.

Begin at Mistley Station, turn left onto the main road and you'll soon see a sign that points left through the back of a factory. Keep within the narrow painted lines and watch out for delivery lorries as you make your way straight down the hill and through the metal gate at the foot.

Turn right and then left, going under the railway track and down the steps to the field below. Head over to the country lane, which you cross to another field. At the gap, turn left and head into the woods. This is Furze Hill and as you head on through the trees up on your left you'll see the impressive Old Knobbley, an 800-year-old oak tree where women used to hide out from the Witchfinder General.

Carry on, keeping the playing fields on your left, until you come out into the open next to a modern housing development. Walk along this path until the end and where it bears left go through the small opening in the hedgerow, which brings you out onto Heath Road. Turn right and go round the corner, where you'll see a gate immediately next to a house on your left. Go through this and

◀ Old Knobbley at Furze Hill, Mistley

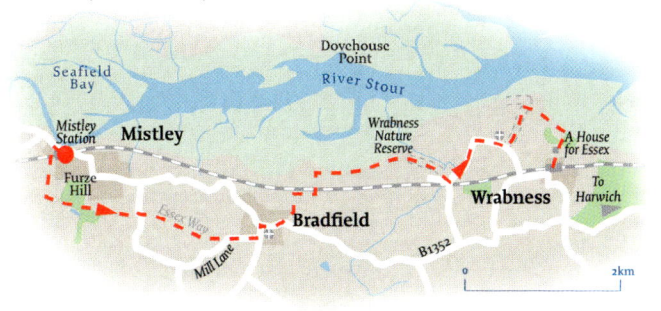

keep going through another gate to a field. Walk all the way across this field and then two more fields, continuing in a straight line as far as possible.

At the bottom of the last field, there's a wooden gate which leads into Mill Lane. This then takes you up and into the village of Bradfield. At the end of the lane, turn left and carry on to the church, where you turn right and then cross over.

At the corner of the Z-bend, there's a footpath off to your left which leads through more fields down to the edge of the railway track. Turn right, then left under the railway bridge before going straight over the fields to reach the saltmarsh sea wall of the Stour Estuary.

Turn right to head along the saltmarsh into Wrabness Nature Reserve, before going left onto the main tarmac path which winds round to a zigzag path. Go down this, turning briefly left at the end of the zigzags, then immediately right onto the wide track that leads to the reserve's car park.

Turn left and then left again onto Wheatsheaf Lane, which winds its way round and into Church Road. Soon after passing the church, go left down Stone Lane. As you head down to the estuary again, look over the field to get your first view of Perry's A House for Essex.

Clad in 2000 handmade tiles and decorated with original sculptures, the remarkable gold-roofed building is reminiscent of a Russian Stave church or pilgrimage chapel but is actually a flamboyant memorial to a fictional character – a woman called Julie Cope – whose imagined life story represents the history of Essex. The house is available as a holiday let and not open to the public.

At the bottom of the lane turn right behind the backs of the riverfront huts and head along to the sea wall, where the views of the river are at their best.

Before you get to the woods, head right up the hill where you really get an up-close view of the House. At the top of the lane, head round to the right where you'll see the car park for Wrabness Station.

# Walton-on-the-Naze

**Distance** 6km **Time** 2 hours **Terrain** grassland, sea wall, town pavements, beach **Map** OS Explorer 184 **Access** buses to Walton-on-the-Naze from Colchester and Clacton; Walton Railway Station is 2.5km from the start

The Naze is a promontory just north of the seaside town of Walton. It takes its name from the Old English *Ness*, meaning 'headland', and is almost surrounded by water with Hamford Water to the west and the sea to the east. A Site of Special Scientific Interest, it was also the setting for one of Arthur Ransome's popular Swallows and Amazons books and has the glorious Naze Tower, built by Trinity House as a navigation aid for ships.

Start from the Naze Nature Discovery Centre, run by Essex Wildlife Trust, and carry on past the navigational tower, which was built in 1720 and at 26m high offers up spectacular 360-degree views. Across the grassland, continue through the patches of gorse, which are at their best in spring when the yellow flowers are dazzling and their telltale coconut aroma fills the air.

At the infantry pillbox, one of the remnants from the Second World War defences that haven't fallen over the clifftops, head right, taking the path that goes through trees and then eventually skirts the cliffs, although these are a lot smaller here than they are back by the Nature Discovery Centre.

This path eventually leads down to the sea wall at the most northeasterly part of the headland, called Stone Point. There's a lovely beach here which surrounds a little lagoon, depending on tide heights. In the distance you should be able to see one of the largest container ports in Europe, Felixstowe, with its rows of cranes that look a little like headless giraffes taking a drink at the local watering hole.

From the sea wall, turn left and carry on around on the path. You'll see that this is a permissive path, so make sure you keep on the sea wall and don't stray onto the farmland below, although with sweeping views over the saltmarshes and the islands of Hamford Water from the wall, there's little reason to. This is where Arthur Ransome, when he lived near Pin Mill on the Shotley Peninsula, set *Secret Water*, the eighth book in his Swallows and Amazons series. As you wander around, look out for a dinghy or two, as well as larger yachts either heading out to sea or back to Titchmarsh Marina, the moored masts of which you can see from the sea wall as you get closer to Walton.

Eventually, you come to a grand nautically painted houseboat and the edge of a caravan park where you need to head left down a dirt path that brings you out onto Hall Lane. Cross to the art deco home on the corner and then walk up the hill back to the Naze. Keep to the pavement beside the tree-lined green spaces until you get to the greensward and playground on your right, which you cross and then take the steps down to the beach between the beach huts. Head left and stay on the promenade rather than the beach itself as to follow the sand would mean having to take the steps up and down to bypass the groynes at various intervals.

This brings you to just before Crag Walk, the coastal defence structure put in place to save the Naze Tower from toppling over the cliffs. Go up the steps and you'll be back at the Naze Nature Discovery Centre.

Beach huts at Walton-on-the-Naze

# Harwich to Dovercourt

**Distance** 4km **Time** 1 hour
**Terrain** promenade and pavement
**Map** OS Explorer 184 **Access** regular buses and trains to Harwich from Colchester

You get more than just beautiful seascapes on this walk through Harwich, it's also fantastically rich in history. It was the home of Christopher Jones, the Captain of the *Mayflower* which took the Pilgrims to America, where they founded a colony that turned into a nation. It also has the country's only original double treadwheel crane (that you can walk inside) and one of the oldest purpose-built cinemas, the Electric Palace, opened in 1911, which still has its original silent screen and projection room.

Start from the loop just outside Harwich Old Town Station and head out to the main road. Turn left and then cross the road to the High Lighthouse, taking care to watch out for traffic. Built in 1818, Harwich's brick lighthouses became redundant in 1863 due to the changing course of the channel, though the High Lighthouse was still used by mariners as a landmark. Continue in the same direction, then turn right down Wellington Road before bearing left into Church Street.

As you walk down this narrow thoroughfare, one of many that crisscross the Old Town, you'll pass the impressive St Nicholas Church on your right and then the equally imposing Town Council Offices on your left. About halfway up, take a right turn down Market Street and then a left down Kings Head Street where you'll find the atmospheric Alma Inn and just across the road the home of Christopher Jones.

At the end of the road, you'll see the Quay and the glorious sight of Harwich Promenade. For the best views, cross the road, and then head right towards the Ha'Penny Pier, built in 1853 as a departure point for paddle steamers. Just past the

# HARWICH TO DOVERCOURT

◀ The Kindertransport Memorial

pier, you'll see the LV 18 Lightvessel and on the promenade the memorial to the Kindertransport programme which rescued more than 10,000 children from Nazi persecution, their main port of entry from Europe being Harwich.

Follow the road round into Kings Quay Street and then straight on at the corner. Just past the stunning façade of the Electric Palace, turn left down Cow Lane and across into Angelgate past the Lifeboat Museum to the beachside promenade where you turn right. Carry on along the main seafront path with views across the harbour to Felixstowe and on the other side the site of the Treadwheel Crane.

The path continues past the Low Lighthouse, which now houses the town's Maritime Museum, and alongside the waterline until it rounds the Beacon Hill spur, where Harwich Harbour meets the open sea and you can see Dovercourt Beach stretching out in front with its striking cast-iron Dovercourt High and Low Lighthouses, built in 1863 to replace those you've already passed.

Past some beach huts and several paths leading up to the roads above, take the diagonal path that passes what was once a toilet block but is now a café and bar. This path steadily climbs to the top of the cliff where on the right it goes under a bridge. Take the next road on the right, Empire Road, and at a sharp corner continue on the unmade track into Kingsway where you turn left past Kingsway Hall, the former Victorian church, now a theatre, down to Dovercourt's High Street.

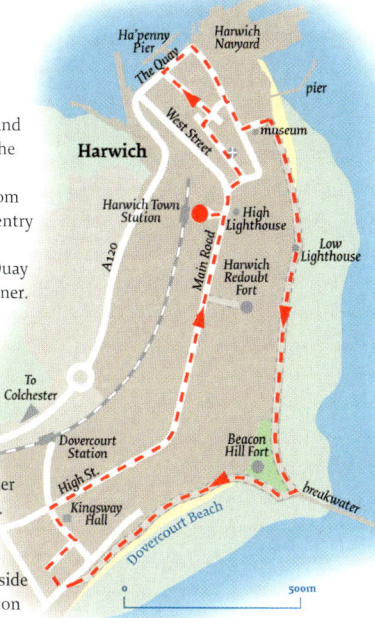

Turn right to head back into Harwich Old Town which at first runs past lines of shops, then passes Cliff Park before it rounds a corner. Just past Mayflower Avenue and between a line of unassuming houses, there's a single track on the right that leads up to Harwich's Redoubt Fort, built to protect against a possible Napoleonic invasion.

The road eventually brings you back into Harwich to the start.

# Index

| | |
|---|---|
| Alresford | 88 |
| Althorne | 70 |
| Audley End House | 8 |
| Basildon | 52 |
| Bradfield | 90 |
| Bradwell-on-Sea | 68 |
| Braintree | 30 |
| Broomway, The | 76 |
| Buckhurst Hill | 20 |
| Burnham | 70 |
| Canvey Island | 54 |
| Castle Hedingham | 26 |
| Chalkwell Beach | 58 |
| Chelmsford | 36 |
| Chipping Ongar | 16 |
| Coalhouse Fort | 48 |
| Coggeshall | 80 |
| Colchester | 84 |
| Colne Valley | 26 |
| Danbury | 38 |
| Dovercourt | 94 |
| East Tilbury | 48 |
| Epping Forest | 18 |
| Finchingfield | 28 |
| Flitch Way | 30 |
| Fobbing | 50 |
| Fordham Heath | 82 |
| Foulness Island | 76 |
| Great Bardfield | 28 |
| Great Waltham | 34 |
| Hadleigh | 56 |
| Harlow Mill | 14 |
| Harwich | 94 |
| Hatfield Forest | 12 |
| Heybridge Basin | 64 |
| Hullbridge | 72 |
| Ingatestone | 40 |
| Langdon Nature Discovery Park | 52 |
| Leigh-on-Sea | 56, 58 |
| Maldon | 66 |
| Mersea Island | 86 |
| Mistley | 90 |
| Pleshey | 34 |
| Plotlands | 52 |
| Purfleet | 44 |
| Queen Elizabeth's Hunting Lodge | 20 |
| Rainham | 44 |
| Rayne | 30 |
| Rochford | 74 |
| Roydon | 14 |
| Saffron Walden | 8 |
| St Botolph's Priory | 84 |
| Snaresbrook | 20 |
| Southend | 58 |
| Terling | 32 |
| Thaxted | 10 |
| Thorndon Country Park | 22 |
| Tilbury Fort | 46 |
| Tollesbury | 62 |
| Wakering Stairs | 76 |
| Walton-on-the-Naze | 92 |
| West Bergholt | 82 |
| West Mersea | 86 |
| White Notley | 32 |
| Wivenhoe | 88 |
| Wrabness | 90 |